funky
STYLE

We can count on a

world that has

learned and digested a

new idea of universality

and discretion in furniture,

literature, religion and music alike.

PAOLA ANTONELLI, MUSEUM OF MODERN ART, NEW YORK

funky STYLE

creative ideas for the contemporary home

NATALIA MARSHALL

with special photography by Chris Tubbs

published in association with

Livingetc

THE MODERN HOME & LIFESTYLE MAGAZINE

WARD LOCK
LONDON

contents

What is Funky?

Modernity now is a bit
like pop music – it's all about
remix, taking an original, then
redoing it in a new material.

FERRUCCIO LAVIANI, FURNITURE DESIGNER

Funky styling is a comfortable approach to home making, very much in keeping with the current spirit of globalism and eclecticism, so visible in our fashion, our food and our music.

Funky is a hybrid look; it combines the old and the new, the fun and the functional, the East and the West. It's about low-maintenance, relaxed, modular and flexible living, where you can change a room's look and role by switching around your furniture or applying a new coat of paint. The ethos of this approach is that good interior style should be accessible to everyone, no matter what the budget. As such, it allows you to build on what you have, while adding items that will bring an inventive, fresh and personal touch to your home. There's always room for excellent, classic design, but being funky also means embracing the kitsch, the witty, and the treasured ephemera of your life.

The funky look is closely aligned to fashion, where design innovations have slowed down, and instead new materials, finishes and fibres give re-invented styles a twist. Colours are bright and hi-energy or muted and sludgy, and shapes are streamlined and organic, anthropomorphic and asymmetrical to enable you to make a bold statement in your living space.

In essence, the funky home is a melting pot of happily unrelated items, picked up from markets, second-hand stores, trips abroad, collectors' fairs and art shows, or even made at home from interesting materials that you have sourced from specialist suppliers.

The key influences are the Modern designs of the 1950s that embraced mass-production and functional forms, the geometric patterns and Pop Art of the 1960s and the disco glamour and hi-tech influences of the 1970s. The effect is that moulded plastic and plywood seating with angular steel legs sit in acid bright settings with industrial-style metal or rubber flooring, and accessorized with bold patterns and glitter finishes. This creates a clashing aesthetic that breaks style barriers yet is totally compelling.

Key trends

There are a few key trends featured on the following pages that epitomize the best of funky, which can be used as a basis for creating your own highly idiosyncratic living space.

Harness the elements that appeal to you and don't be afraid to create new combinations with pattern and texture, shape and colour. Customize anything you own that does not fit in with your fledgling look. The funky style seeker needs to be a jackdaw, a dedicated re-cycler, a re-packager, a scavenger and a shameless collector of anything that the less discerning interior decorator would pass over. Look for possibilities in anything unusual, old, discarded or interesting. Use materials that are out of the ordinary, or use mundane materials in extraordinary ways. Traditional haberdashers, hardware stores, stationers, Oriental stores and artists' shops can yield all kinds of effects from aluminium or bronze leaf to handmade paper, textured glass and unusual or imitation paint finishes, to fabrics, ribbons, tissue and giftwrap, beads, buttons, and labels.

The look is certainly eclectic, but the end result should not be chaos. Although there are few rules, the practical advice in the pages of this book will help you achieve fusion rather than confusion. This is one style that can't be slavishly copied, relying as it does on adapting and customizing and following your instincts. It is constantly changing, evolving and modifying with you. So throw yourself into it, be creative, be confident, and above all, have fun.

Technological advances have introduced intense colours in lightweight plastics that inject vitality into the dullest of household objects. The theme is continued in wall paints and upholstery.

Hi-energy

plastic

polypropylene

acrylic

lime

tangerine

lemon

fuchsia

The enduring sleek, modern look of metal appliances and gadgets has been extended to the new metallic finishes in fabrics, paints and wallpapers.

Metallic

aluminium

steel

chrome

zinc

bronze

pearly

glitter

reflective

shiny

Sensuous and extravagant, fur (both real and fake) is stylish once again, and the longer the pile the better, together with anything bobbly, woolly, fluffy and smooth. The funky home is filled with objects you just want to reach out and touch.

Tactile

leather

suede

sheepskin

feathers

microfibre

shagpile

fur

The sentimental and the gaudy can now be celebrated. Dig out your bits and pieces and display them with panache and humour.

14   FUNKY STYLE

Kitsch

inflatables

fruit

Eastern

pets

pinks

embroidery

lanterns

imitation

cartoons

tassels

The popular and pioneering designs of yester-year form the basis of funky styling, mixing genuine and imitation pieces.

Retro

circles

Pop Art

psychedelia

organic shapes

moulded plastics

chrome

geometric prints

leather

space-age

abstract art

gingham

colour

Colour sets the tone of the funky home, whether you want to head for the brash end of the funky spectrum in all-out primaries and acid brights, or create a restrained atmosphere, where baby blues and lemon yellows form a backdrop against which to show off the organic shapes of modern furniture and collections of accessories. Get ready to try chocolate brown, cool beige and serene grey – so long rejected as suitable colours for interior design. Now it's time to throw out all existing prejudices and try all sorts of new and exciting combinations.

A Clever Colour Scheme

Step into any good decorating store and you're confronted by row upon row of paint swatches in every conceivable shade. Never has the choice of colours for the home been so good, as varied and so dazzling, but the flip side of having so many tempting tones is that making the right choice can be a real challenge.

Glancing through glossy interiors magazines only adds to the confusion, crammed as they are with fabulous homes decked out in exotic shades of citrus orange and lime, purple, and – in these days of fascination with all things retro – beige and brown. It's inspiring when it's in other people's homes – but what about your own? How do you get that seemingly effortless colour success?

As with so many other things, it's largely a question of choosing something that suits you, that suits your lifestyle – and furnishings, if you have them – and that creates the feeling you want from a particular room. But a little basic colour science can go a long way in helping you get the balance right, while achieving a truly individual look.

LEFT The citrus yellow-green of the walls here is accentuated by the raspberry wall lights and deep purple curtains. This scheme works because of the room's minimal and unfussy furnishings and accessories, mostly in muted colours, that really bring out the richness of the colours.

105652.

RIGHT This bold colour scheme for a kitchen is uplifting despite the choice of a deep blue for the ceiling. Height is emphasized by the yellow and pale blue walls, and the unusual curved units help to break up the blocks of colour, so that the overall scheme works brilliantly.

BELOW A bright lofty shade of green injects instant impact in a hallway.

Setting the tone

As the largest surface area in a room, the colour (or colours) you choose for your walls is crucially important when it comes to setting the mood for that room. A day with a paintbrush can transform a dull kitchen into a fresh one, or a gloomy living room into a vibrant one.
It's great to rifle through other people's ideas on colour scheming, but ultimately what it comes down to is how certain colours make you feel – it's an emotional as well as a practical decision.

For instance, wall-to-wall tangerine may make one person feel zesty and alive, but on a more nervous individual it may make them jittery or overwhelmed. The current mood for eclecticism is great, as it basically means anything goes (so long as it's done well and with the right accessories and furnishings).

A little confidence goes a long way when it comes to colour combining, but if you need some help, most of the big paint manufacturers are now grouping their colours together in moods, on the basis that any colours from one group will combine successfully, thus helping you to create a room that is either warm or cool, refreshing or vivid.

Where to start

Your starting point must be to assess what you already have in terms of furniture or large accessories. If you have a sofa, a picture, a pair of curtains or a rug you're into, try picking out one of the colours it contains as a starting point, and build up your colour scheme from there. But make sure you know what kind of mood you're after. What is going to make you happy? Is it a room to chill out in, a room to be creative in or a room to wake up and get energized in? Is it an adults-only room, or a family room? Will you mainly use it in the evening or during the day? The colours you choose will play a key role in generating this mood.

You also need to consider how the room is lit from outside. A bright, south-facing room with massive windows has a completely different feel to one that faces north or has tiny windows. Equally, at night, the kind of lighting you have can transform both the atmosphere and the colours (see Chapter 4).

ABOVE LEFT Emulate the current art trend for all things circular and have a go yourself using this simple abstract design. Try aubergine with acid yellow, orange with turquoise, cerise with lime green or coffee with cream. One sure guarantee of success is to use a gradation of tones, one of which matches your wall colour. (See pages 34-35 for details.)

ABOVE A well designed piece of furniture in a bold colour is a good starting paint around which to organize your colour scheme.

LEFT With colours like these, you really don't need much else in a room. This ultra-simple scheme works especially well because although two contrasting colours are used, they are similar tonally so one does not dominate. The turquoise wall colour is continued over existing features, such as the tongue and groove panelling and picture rail, to maximize the sense of height and continuity.

Get it in proportion

When it comes to deciding how many colours to incorporate into your colour scheme it is worth remembering that two colours used in exactly the same proportion can end up looking either busy or indecisive. So for a more fluid scheme, use just one dominant colour to cover the majority of the wall space, and make up the balance with one or more shades. Other colours could go into the woodwork, on the ceiling, below the dado rail if you have one, or even on just one wall or an alcove, and be picked up in the furnishings and fittings.

A useful exercise when deciding on your dominant colour is to rifle through lots of swatches, narrow the choice down to a handful that truly appeal to you and get tester pots for each. Paint generous-sized swatches on the walls, or paint large pieces of cardboard and move them around the room so you can see how the colour looks in different lights. Don't make a final decision right away; live with your swatches for a day or two and see if you still like them. Put existing furnishings next to them and see how they go together – any serious clashes will show straight away.

RIGHT A restrained scheme of brown, cream and maroon is warm and relaxing, but has a couple of twists to create interest. The alcove is painted in dark chocolate, a colour that is repeated in the 60s-style fabric carefully folded across a thin pole to make the simplest of blinds.

Colour combining

Once you've chosen your dominant colour, you'll need to think about other shades – woodwork, for instance, the ceiling, or you may even opt for an above and below dado rail scheme. And this is the hard part: mix in the wrong shade and you'll kill your carefully chosen dominant colour. One guideline that is easy to follow is to check that the tone and intensity of co-habiting colours match. If you're not sure about this, look at paint swatches in the store. They are arranged not only by colour, but also by the amount of black and white pigment that has been mixed in. So paler tones, the ones with the most white in, sit at the top, and the deeper, intense shades are at the bottom. Choose colours that come roughly from the same area. If you want to go all out for strong primary colours it is better to use not more than four, and use bright accessories as colour accents.

ABOVE There are plenty of kitchen accessories that belong in the funky club. Just make them big, bright and beautiful.

OPPOSITE This kitchen is full of glorious primaries, but there's enough pale wood in the units to prevent it becoming overwhelming. The combination works because the colours are all of the same intensity.

BELOW No kitchen should be without a cordless phone. Get one that matches your colour scheme.

ABOVE Kitchen appliances can no longer be called white goods, when they come in such an astonishing array of colours and finishes, like this cobalt blue refrigerator.

LEFT Accessorize in a bright colourful kitchen with a yellow expresso machine.

Soft, challenging or all-in-ones?

There are basically three ways of combining colours – contrasting, blending and harmonizing. Contrasting colour schemes are among the most exciting, although a certain amount of experimentation is inevitable before it comes just right. Use colours that are at opposite ends of the spectrum such as fuchsia pink with black and white, or deep purple with acid yellow. Blending or monochromatic colour schemes are easy on the eye and ideal if you find choosing colours difficult, as they use just one colour as the basis. Interest is created by adding in graded shades of that colour. If you want to be a little more adventurous, you could throw the whole thing into focus by introducing an accent colour in tiny quantities: a chocolate brown cushion against lime green perhaps, or a crimson throw in a pale blue bedroom. Harmonizing colour schemes are fairly straightforward to put together, and use two or three colours close to each other on the colour spectrum. For example, you could combine warm colours such as such as yellows, ochres and oranges or go cool with turquoises, blues and lilacs.

Going white

White is not a colour that is immediately associated with funky style, but it can provide a clean, fresh backdrop that will allow the dramatic shapes, bold designs and luxurious textures of your furniture and accessories to take centre stage. Try to avoid brilliant white, as this can look harsh, particularly in north temperate zones. Instead go for off-white shades of chalk, eggshell, and barely-there beige.

Grey is another option that is becoming increasingly popular. Make a statement by choosing one or two cool grey tones for your walls and lifting the overall scheme with accents of shocking pink, luscious green and tangy orange.

Whatever colour scheme you choose, it's best to rely on your own instinct. When all's said and done, it's as much about personal taste as anything. If a particular combination makes you feel good, throw all the rules out of the window and go for it. Be brave and adventurous, but above all go for something that gives you lots of positive energy.

OPPOSITE It doesn't have to be bright to be funky. In an all-white setting, attention is drawn to the mantlepiece and the quirky display of ephemera.

RIGHT Pale walls are the perfect complement to the minimalist feel of this urban living room, accentuating all the available light and space.

STYLE POINTERS

Choose colours that make you feel good.

Experiment with the biggest swatches you can before you get painting. Remember that a whole room painted in a colour is likely to appear around three shades stronger than in a tiny sample.

The amount and quality of light in a room affects colour dramatically, so choose your colour scheme according to the time of day that the room will be most used.

Generally speaking, warm colours such as oranges, reds and yellows 'advance' making a room feel smaller and more cozy, while cool colours such as greens, blues and greys 'recede', opening a room and making it feel more spacious.

South facing and sunny rooms can get hot and stuffy in the summer. They can be 'cooled' with soft green, aqua or lilac, or fresh shades such as lemon and fuchsia. North facing rooms, on the other hand, lend themselves well to warm, vibrant colours such as honey yellow, terracotta and dusty pink.

Employ a little colour psychology – colours have different wavelengths and affect our retinas in varying ways. Bright red has long wavelengths and requires our eyes to adjust a lot, so some people find a whole room in red claustrophobic. Green, by contrast, with its short wavelengths, is more easy on the eye and restful.

Associations are important, too. Think of the openness of the wide blue sky, the relaxing power of the turquoise sea or the warmth of a yellow summer sun.

RIGHT Take inspiration from your favourite movie or TV show. This red hallway is reminiscent of the dream sequence from *Twin Peaks*.

Dealing with problem areas

Few of us are perfect – we all have our own endearing quirks and imperfections – and the same is true of our homes. Many rooms are too narrow, poky, dark or awkwardly shaped. And in the same way as you might change your hair colour or apply your brightest and best Chanel lipstick, this is the time to think about using colour to disguise those less than perfect characteristics. There are few rooms, no matter how strangely proportioned, that can't be helped by the right colour scheme. Try some of the following solutions:

BELOW: Wake up each morning to a fresh, bright bedroom. Sorbet colours are invigorating and clean, and work well with a low-maintenance easy-going room.

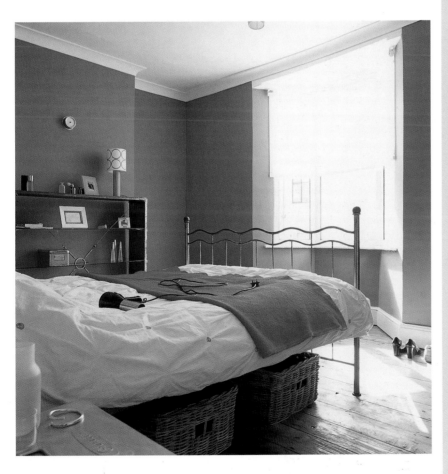

LOW CEILINGS

Use a pale colour such as off-white or light blue that will recede and make the ceiling seem higher. Contrast with a darker colour on the walls. You can also extend the wall colour up into the cornicing if you have it, and down to the skirting board to make the walls seem higher, or paint architectural details such as dado and picture rails the same colour as the walls to give an impression of continuity.

AWKWARDLY SHAPED ROOMS

You can use strong, advancing colours to alter a room's proportions; for instance in an L-shaped room painting the short and long walls opposite the same colour to link them. Loft rooms with sloping roofs can look very odd and it can be hard to see where the ceiling ends and wall begins. Get round this by painting the whole room in one colour. Use vinyl silk emulsion paint as this has a subtle sheen that reflects light.

SMALL ROOMS

Painting a cramped room white is an obvious solution, but you could also try cool, receding shades such as violet, pale blue or soft yellow. The same goes for the floor – choose a pale-coloured floor covering and paint the skirting board in the closest matching shade you can find to make the floor area – and so the entire room – seem larger.

NARROW ROOMS AND HALLWAYS

Make a room seem wider with strong, horizontal lines or patterns, ideally in warm, advancing colours. Try applying a lighter colour below the dado rail level to create a horizontal line around a room and emphasize its width. Paint the two shortest walls the same advancing colour so that they appear to 'meet', while the longest walls should stay in a pale, receding colour.

circle artwork

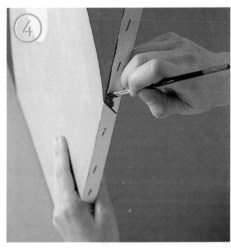

1 Place the bowl in the bottom left-hand corner of the canvas, so that it cuts into the canvas as far as you want and paint around it in lime green paint using a small artist's brush.

2 Along the diagonal from this corner to the top right-hand corner, place the cup within the painted circular outline. Paint around it in apple green using another small artist's brush. Place the cup so that it cuts into the canvas at the top right-hand corner and paint an outline around this edge in apple green.

3 Paint the main circle with the lime green paint and leave to dry. Paint a second coat and leave to dry. Give the two small circles two coats of apple green allowing the paint to dry between coats. With the larger paintbrush, give the remaining canvas two coats of aubergine, allowing the paint to dry between coats.

4 Paint down over the edge of the canvas by continuing the relevant colours using the small brushes.

Materials

50 × 60cm/19³/₄ × 23⁵/₈in ready stretched canvas (available from artists' suppliers)
Large round bowl or plate
Small cup or jar
Small artist's brushes
1.5cm/²/₃in paintbrush

Tester pot of apple green (Dulux 0050-G40Y) water-based paint
Tester pot of lime green (Dulux 0080-G40Y) water-based paint
Tester pot of aubergine (Dulux 6030-R50B) water-based paint

TIPS Painting long, fast strokes gives a smoother line to the circles, but don't worry about getting the edges perfect – wobbly lines are fine. Wait until each circle is completely dry before doing the next to avoid blotching. Do a rough first on a piece of paper if you're not confident. You can use any colours you like, but to play safe make one colour the same shade as your wall, one a couple of shades darker and one a couple of shades lighter.

paint effects

Committed funksters may well shudder at the words 'paint effects' as images of rag-rolling, dragging and sponging spring to mind. But paint effects can be cool, as long as they are kept simple and clean – no textures please! Think of your interior walls as more than just somewhere to hang pictures. They are a canvas for your creativity, to be decorated in numbers, letters, circles, lines and stripes in the new generation metallic, glitter and pearlized paints. Break with convention, show some audacity and place them somewhere unexpected, in nooks and crannies and incorporate existing architectural features. Try your hand with sample pots first, and if you feel nervous about the finished result, restrict your painting to just one wall. But draw them out with bold shapes; run circles around fireplaces and numbers around light switches. Precise symmetry isn't essential – play around with different angles, heights and proportions.

Stripes

Horizontal or vertical stripes in the right place can be highly effective, but need to be done well – or at least assertively. Decorating books will tell you that horizontal stripes have the effect of making walls seem shorter, whereas vertical stripes make a room look taller, but if you limit yourself to pale colours, you should avoid much shrinking and expanding. Stripes in darker or brighter colours are enjoyed most by people who don't mind feeling dizzy and hemmed in.

If you have a fairly steady hand you could try applying the stripes by hand (draw them in pencil first), which gives a freeform soft-edged look. Otherwise, and if your walls are sound, use low-tack masking tape to mark out the stripes. Use a spirit level to ensure they stay straight. If your stripes are alternate light and

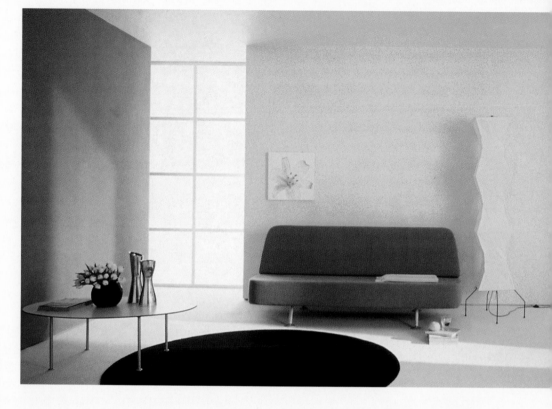

dark, you will find it easier if you paint the whole wall in the lighter colour first, then paint the darker coloured stripes over the top when this coat is completely dry.

For a subtle, and far easier effect, try a single horizontal band of paint in a different colour to the wall that runs all the way round the room above the picture rail, skirting board or at dado rail height. It can be as wide or as narrow as you feel is appropriate.

Blocks

Geometric shapes are so versatile because they can fit together to create an entirely new effect. A simple version of this involves painting each wall of a room in varying tones of the same

colour. For a more dramatic finish on a wall that does not have a window, divide the surface into four or six blocks and paint each one a different shade. This can also be done on a smaller scale using coloured squares or rectangles to make up a larger shape.

ABOVE Large screens painted in reflective paints have such a glorious luminous sheen, that little additional decoration is required.

LEFT Stripes in cereal shades produce a pleasing asymmetry in a design that incorporates the picture frame.

OPPOSITE If you haven't got quite the right picture, make one yourself, by painting rectangles directly onto the wall.

Lines

A single line running either vertically or horizontally is very simple to do, yet can have great impact. Create the illusion of a vertical line at the meeting point of two different wall colours half way along one wall rather than at the corner. Alternatively, use a dark shade to demarcate the meeting point of two paler colours. This device can act as a visual punctuation mark to divide two separate functions of a room, such as a dining or office area from a lounge area. The effect can be done just the same as for stripes, using masking tape, or if it is a thin line you want, you could just use one strip of tape, and use this as a straight edge along which to paint.

Letters & numbers

This is where you can get plenty of effect for the minimum amount of effort. You can make simple stencils by enlarging images on a photocopier (make sure each sits in the middle of the paper) and cutting out the shapes, ideally with a scalpel for a razor-sharp edge. For extra strength, glue the paper stencils to cardboard and cut out. Leaf through magazines or books from the 60s or 70s for some funky retro typefaces, so evocative of childhood books and comics, detective and sci-fi novels, or take a trip to your local stationer's or art suppliers for contemporary stencils and Letrasets. If you have access to a PC, you can print out your chosen letters from its supply of fonts and then enlarge them.

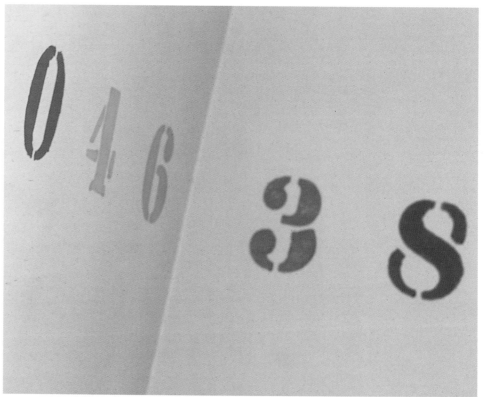

ABOVE Red and yellow meet and jostle for supremacy in a line that runs at an angle.

RIGHT Paint a random order of numbers with antique printers plates around the corner of a room, or pick out important dates such as anniversaries. (See pages 44-45 for details.)

OPPOSITE For the ultimate paint effect in a nursery or children's room, use dots to form letters of the alphabet.

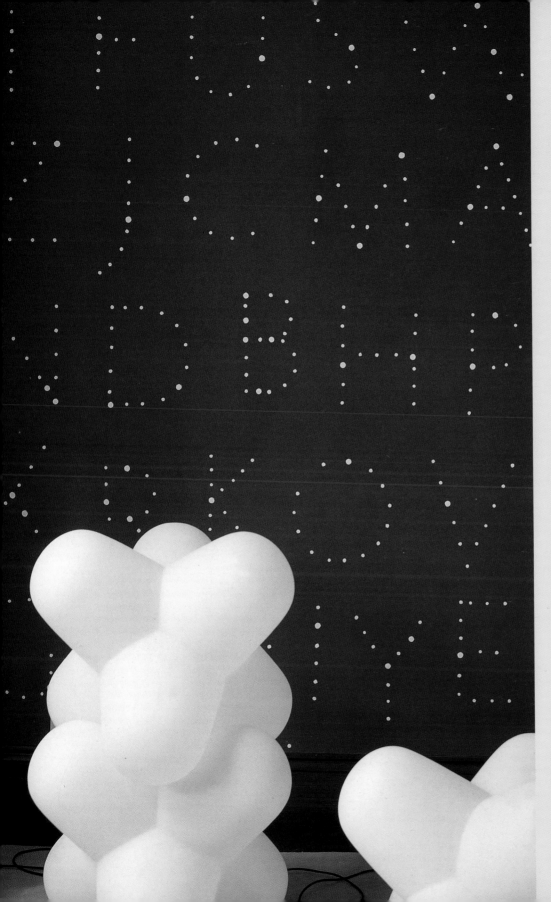

Circles

Circles, such as those pictured on page 36, are quite time-consuming to draw out, but worth the effort for that evocative 60s feel. To achieve the same result, you have to measure out a grid on the wall using a pencil, metal tape measure and spirit level. Covering a whole wall, and in soft shades, the end result is very satisfying. If you want to pursue a random arrangement, it is better to cover a smaller area of wall. Small monotone circle stencils make a mischievous paint effect running round a wall at skirting board height.

Metallic, pearlized, glitter & fluorescent

For a touch of disco glamour, try dabbling in the frivolous range of metallic, pearlized and glitter paints that are available today. You can choose from sugary pastels to luminous green or yellow, rich exotic golds to silver, bronze and copper. You may not want to paint an entire room in these special finishes, but any of the paint effects previously mentioned would have great impact. Moderation is definitely the key to success. If you want to be really experimental, you could try covering part of a wall with silver or aluminium leaf, which comes in the form of sheets of rub-down transfer, usually sold in packs of twenty-five. It's a bit difficult to apply, but can look brilliant.

1. Green hammered metallic.
2. Fluorescent green.
3. Blue glitter.
4. Purple metallic.
5. Gold metallic.
6. Pink pearlized.
7. Silver glitter.
8. Silver metallic.
9. Fluorescent yellow.
10. Bronze metallic.
11. Fluorescent pink.
12. Cobalt blue metallic.

stencilled numbers

1 Line up the spirit level at the desired height along the wall to ensure that you get a straight line.
2 Draw a faint line in pencil to act as a guide along the top of the spirit level.
3 Take a stencil and rest the bottom on the line. With a gentle stippling motion, dab the paint onto the stencil. Continue along the wall stencilling using the numbers and the paints in a random order.
4 When the paint is completely dry (wait around three hours) carefully rub out the pencil line.

Materials

Tester pot of olive green
   (Dulux 3060-G90Y) paint
Tester pot of mustard yellow
   (Dulux 1060-G90Y) paint
Tester pot of red
   (Dulux 1777-Y81R) paint
Number stencils

Stippling brushes
Ruler
Pencil
Eraser
Spirit level

TIPS The brush's bristles should be barely coated with paint and the stencil must be kept absolutely still to avoid ugly blobs. I used antique printers numbers, but you could make your own stencils from stiff cardboard featuring small circles, squares or other simple shapes. Avoid using primary colours if you don't want your room to look like a nursery.

flooring

The floor area offers great potential for experimentation and innovation. Carpet is quiet and indulgent, but there are so many other coverings on offer – many of which have migrated from industrial settings – that are practical and hardwearing, and are perfect for the modern aesthetic. There are practical considerations, such as whether you have children and therefore need flooring that is particularly resilient and easy to clean, whether you live in a flat and need noise-absorbing underlay, or whether you already have wooden floorboards that are in good condition and only need a light sanding and varnishing. Virtually any kind of flooring lends itself to a modern look, depending on its treatment.

Funky Floors

When it comes to home basics, what you walk on is just as important as what you hang your pictures on. It may be a cliché to say that the floor is the fifth wall, but it certainly does cover a large surface area and as such it needs a lot of attention, and a lot of thought when you are considering the other elements of your interior style.

When you move into a new house or apartment, you may find yourself dealing with flooring that has been down for decades. Before you pull it up, check its condition. Linoleum that was laid in the 70s should still be in great shape, and is now considered the height of good taste. It may not be in the strong energizing colours of today's marketplace, but try to work with it rather than pulling it up.

Classic can sit happily with modern – the combination is a characteristic component of the funky look – so before you strip antique floorboards, or rip out elegant parquet or pale slate, consider how you can bring their inherent qualities into your funky style. Work them into your colour scheme or make a design statement out of their worn appearance.

LEFT Old and new merge as a modern carpet is anchored over painted old floorboards with a metal trim.

RIGHT If you're lucky enough to live in a house or apartment that retains its original tesselated tiles and parquet, it is worth taking some time and effort to keep them looking good, as they provide a stunning backdrop to furnishings and accessories of any style.

Rubber

Rubber is probably the ultimate funky floor. It originally made its way into our homes during the hi-tech period of the late 70s when industrial-style fittings were popular. If you want to pursue the more severe hi-tech look, opt for austere blacks and greys. These can act as superb foils for boldly painted walls. But if you're looking for something a little more cheerful, there is such a vast range of truly stunning colours available nowadays that you will be spoilt for choice. Rubber is excellent for kitchens and bathrooms, but true funksters don't stop there; they use it in living rooms and bedrooms, too. It's warm and soft underfoot, can be cleaned with a swish of detergent, is hardwearing, and shrink, stain and burn resistant. It's anti-static (good for the home office), anti-bacterial, and especially when it comes to the varieties with raised textures of round studs, ribs and grooves, it's all anti-slip. It absorbs noise well, so it's perfect for party animals. Sounds too good to be true? Well, there's more – you can choose from plain, patterned or marbled finishes, and if you can't find the exact colour you want, you can have it specially made. As rubber is commonly sold in tile form, this gives you the added advantage of mixing your colours to create a chequerboard look.

LEFT When polished with a water-soluble wax emulsion, a uniform rubber floor takes on a beautiful glossy sheen with a heightened intensity of colour.

Linoleum

Linoleum is making a big comeback, due to a large extent, to the fact that it is made from natural – and sustainable – materials (linseed oil, chalk, wood flour and pine resin). Technical improvements have also increased the range of colours and patterns that are available. You can now choose from around thirty muted colours and a choice of feature tiles and borders. It has a grainy matt finish, which can be buffed to a glossy sheen. Highly durable, anti-bacterial, smooth and easy to clean, linoleum can be kept dust free with a quick swipe of the mop. It will improve with age, which in a funky home full of objects picked from the whole of the twentieth century serves as a plus point. It's affordable, too, but should always be fitted by a specialist. One disadvantage is that it tends to come in fairly narrow widths, so large rooms end up with a seam running through, but you can get around this by incorporating a pattern.

Vinyl

The notion of vinyl flooring may cause design purists to shudder, but it has moved on from the days of fake terracotta tiles and strange abstract patterns – though of course these are still available if it's the retro 60s look you're after. Now you can find an astonishing range of finishes from specialist manufacturers, as long as you're prepared to pay rather more than for your standard vinyl ranges, such as convincing imitation glass, marble, parquet, mosaic, granite and metal. It even comes with disco-style glitter incorporated onto a background of colours such as mint green, lilac, silver grey and midnight blue. Vinyl is washable, affordable and easy to fit, although not as enduring as either rubber or linoleum.

TOP RIGHT Made from natural yet highly resilient materials, lino comes in a vast range of dynamic colours and is deceptively warm to walk on.

We've been trying

to move on for 20 years,

then suddenly everyone

turns round and says,

hey we liked what was

happening in the 70s!

BARRY GIBB, BEE GEES

Some types of flooring combine the warmth of carpet with the durability and cleanliness of vinyl, and are ideal for small children and pets. One of these is the product Flotex which boasts 66 million nylon fibres in every metre.

Metal

Originally considered suitable only for commercial and industrial settings, metal has become an acceptable domestic flooring. It has a sleek, eye-catching finish that is ideal for the industrial post-modernist look. You may not want it for your living room, but for kitchens, stairways and even bathrooms, it can look very effective. Choose something with a raised pattern to protect against slipping. Metal floors are usually made from aluminium or galvanized steel, and have to be ordered from specialist manufacturers.

Concrete

Concrete is a flooring that is dismissed as harsh and unyielding, yet it can be instantly transformed through screeding and painting, waxing or coating to achieve a stylish, shiny tone. Concrete can be bought as slabs or tiles, or it can be mixed and laid on site. It is usually found only at basement and ground levels as a sub-floor for other floor coverings. Why not take up the upper flooring and check its condition? As long as the surface is not crumbly, chalky or loose, you can use a couple of coats of ordinary emulsion or paint topped off with two or three coats of fast-drying acrylic varnish to give it a beautiful finish. As concrete is absorbent the finished effect will be pleasantly faded. You can also use special floor paint, but it's not quite so environmentally friendly. If you do want to have a concrete floor put down, you could always embed other materials such as pebbles into it before it sets, then seal and wax. If you are planning to lay a material like cork tiles over it, you will need to seal the concrete first with a PVA/water solution. Laminate and wooden overlays won't require sealing, but if your floor is in the least bit uneven it will need to be smoothed with a liquid screed or a thin layer of plywood first. Keep concrete clean by scrubbing with hot water and detergent.

Carpet

Until recently eschewed in favour of hard floors such as vinyl and wood, carpet is experiencing something of a revival among the hip, the cold-toed and the 70s wannabes. It may not be as hygienic and easy to clean as other kinds of flooring, but it is worth remembering its more tactile qualities – warm is now cool. There are plenty of varieties that meet the funky criteria. Shagpile for instance, once deemed downmarket and surburban, has been rediscovered by advocates of 60s style. Deep and luxurious with a pile of up to 50mm (2in) long, a shagpile rug in shades of chocolate brown or cream is an essential item for any funky living room.

OPPOSITE After a long absence from the style scene, woollen shagpile carpet can now be seen in the funkiest homes.

RIGHT Achieve industrial chic without feeling a chill underfoot with Amtico's fake metal treadplates that are actually made of vinyl.

ABOVE Metal flooring looks fantastic in a kitchen furnished with metal shelving and shiny appliances.

Colour addicts can look for carpet in such shades as turquoise, orange and citrus yellow. Add a border in a contrasting shade or perhaps an animal print pattern for added zing. Ideally go for 80 per cent wool mixed with 20 per cent man-made fibres such as nylon for the right blend of durability and softness. Then there is the range of natural fibres of sisal, coir, jute and rush that are chosen for their muted shades, loose weaves and nubbly texture. Carpet is not great for damp areas such as bathrooms, so if you're determined to stay soft underfoot stick to carpet tiles.

ABOVE Break down boundaries and bring the garden inside with a 3-D effect imitation floral rug.

BELOW Introduce an instant splash of colour to an otherwise monochrome floor with rugs in abstract patterns.

Sanded floorboards

The simplest and most affordable of all floors, stripped and sanded wooden boards are universally appealing and versatile, and can be done by hiring a floor sander over a weekend if your existing boards are suitable. Add a jolt of colour with a groovy rug, treat them to a muted colour wash, or go all minimalist and simply apply a few coats of clear acrylic varnish.

Strip wood & laminates

A vast expanse of floor shimmering with light-coloured wooden flooring looks so sophisticated. If you can afford it, solid wooden floors such as ash, oak or beech will last for years and are easy to maintain. If you're on a budget, a good quality laminate (thin strips of wood glued onto other materials such as plywood) can look good, too, but don't expect

too much durability – the surface coating tends to wear away after just a couple of years. Wooden floors can also be fitted over a thin layer of insulation, ideal if you need extra sound proofing or warmth. For the ultimate funky wooden floor, you could paint a shape directly onto it as an imitation rug or to demarcate different areas. (See following pages for details.)

ABOVE The natural grain of stripped floorboard brings a understated vitality to this kitchen that is mirrored in the muted pattern of the animal print fabric covering the bar stools.

LEFT Laminated floorboards provide a sleek modern look that can be dressed in any number of ways.

OPPOSITE Plain floorboards are given the funky treatment with a zebra print rug.

circle floor effect

1 Knot the end of a ball of string around a drawing pin and holding the pin lightly in the floor, unravel the string to the desired diameter of your circle. Cut off the length of string and holding it tightly, test the size of your circle.

2 Attach the pencil to the cut end of the string. Holding the drawing pin down firmly with one hand, draw out the circle with the pencil.

3 Sand the floor surface within the circle lightly to provide a key for the paint.

4 Carefully paint within the pencil line in red paint. Allow to dry. Paint a second coat if required. Paint a topcoat of protective water-based varnish to protect the surface.

Materials

Bright red emulsion paint

Medium-sized paintbrush

Sandpaper

Water-based varnish

Pencil

Ball of string

Drawing pin

TIPS Draw out the circle in one fast, sweeping movement so no joins are visible. I used ordinary emulsion paint, plus a protective topcoat of clear fast-drying varnish, but you could also use special floor paint. You can paint a circle onto concrete, or wooden floors. Concrete needs to be sealed first. Floorboards that have already been varnished need a thorough sanding and cleaning with methylated spirits before you start painting.

lighting

Lighting is all too often thought about right at the end of the design process, long after all the other elements have been put into place. But this is a mistake, as good lighting can wonderfully enhance an already successful colour scheme – while poor lighting just as successfully kills it. Imposing floor lamps and stunning chandeliers can provide great focal points, soft accent lighting can alter the mood dramatically, while projected kinetic lighting is the modern answer to firelight – a flickering, ever-changing light to bring life into a room. So do yourself and your home a favour, and think about good lighting early on.

Flexible Lighting

When it comes to lighting, it's all too easy to nip into a trendy store, grab a few lamps then plug in, switch on and chill out. All well and good, as far as it goes, but there are smarter ways to approach this, one of the most important aspects of home design. Stick to a few basic rules and make your lighting really work for you, enhancing moods you want to create, highlighting favourite objects, creating a sparkling focal point or simply providing light to live, play or work by.

There's nothing worse than a powerful bulb right in the centre of a room that casts its unforgiving glare all around and provides absolutely zero atmosphere.

By contrast, the most successful lighting schemes are usually the ones with most flexibility, and this applies to any interior style. Get the lighting right and your room is made – get it wrong and your carefully chosen colour scheme is lifeless. Versatility is key, so install as many dimmer switches as you can, have plenty of portable table lamps, and in dining-cum-kitchen areas have the central pendant light on a long flex so that you can extend it and lower it over the table when you have friends to dinner. Introduce the funky element through coloured bulbs and quirky shapes for your lampshades and bases. There are basically five different kinds of lighting to think about – ambient, accent, task, decorative and kinetic.

ABOVE Just like a doll with different outfits, this little cylindrical design comes with several different paper sheets that can be changed to suit your room. The ultimate flexible lamp.

RIGHT Make your own lampshade out of polypropylene that provides an effervescent glow when lit. The detail is added in the rivets which hold the shade together. Make several in different colours as the perfect finishing touch to a mellow atmosphere. (See pages 68–69 for details.)

RIGHT Add a touch of glitz to your home style with a glorious chandelier. This version mixes coloured with clear glass droplets for a truly glamorous look.

Accent lighting

Once your ambient lighting is in place you can install low-key accent lighting, which can shine onto pictures, plants, ornaments or even architectural details such as recesses. Done well, this creates interesting shadows and reflections, and breathes life and atmosphere into a room. But it's not simply a case of sticking a lamp up against your finest Andy Warhol reproduction: only highlight things that are really worth it, and stick to just a couple of accent lights for greater effect. Try recessed ceiling spots, angle poise lamps and adjustable spotlights.

Ambient lighting

Ambient light is the light that surrounds us, and forms the basis of lighting design. During the day, this light comes naturally from windows and doors, and at night it should come from a bright but well shielded source, ideally a combination of wall lamps or uplighters (small, low voltage fittings set into ceilings or walls), or failing that an overhead ceiling light. You should aim for workable brightness, but avoid anything that gives off glare. Where possible, create a softer feel by directing lights against walls, floors and ceilings rather than directly into a room. Dimmer switches are useful for creating the right mood, too.

Task lighting

Task lighting isn't just for the home office – you need it for everyday jobs such as cooking, reading or writing letters. Ideally task lighting should shine onto the area you are working in or on, highlighting detail, but it shouldn't be so bright that it makes you wince. Find task lights that are adjustable, have shields around the bulbs and have reflectors or lenses to cast light in the direction you want. If you work at a computer, look for a bulb of 60 watts – anything less can cause eye strain. For the kitchen, fit adjustable spots with dimmer switches that can focus on different activities such as eating or cooking. Position strip lights under wall units for cooking without glare.

Decorative lighting

A truly fabulous ceiling, wall or floor lamp can create such a wonderful focal point for a room, that little else is required. Decorative lighting may not be as practical as other kinds, but when you've got a shimmering crystal chandelier, a giant white obelisk or acid-bright plastic cones to admire, who cares? If you can't afford to buy a stunning lamp, it's easy to make your own with a favourite ornament, or customize one you already have to make it a bit different.

Kinetic lighting

Kinetic lighting (from the Greek 'to move') is purely frivolous. It is moving light that brings energy and movement into a room. Kinetic lighting comes in the form of flickering neon lights, amorphous glitter or lava lamps, or simply from twinkling candles and dancing firelight. For a more indirect source, you can hang a revolving disco ball and shine light onto it for a sparkling mobile reflection.

WHICH BULB?

Before you buy a light make sure you know what kind of bulbs it uses. Tungsten bulbs are the commonest kind of bulbs, but have a short life span and are not very energy efficient – although they are affordable and cast a comfortable, yellowish light. Fluorescent bulbs, including the compact kind, are energy efficient and long lived, but can cast a very bright and artificial light and cannot be dimmed. Low-voltage halogen bulbs are reasonably energy efficient, dimmable and give a clear white light that's fairly close to natural light. The bulbs are small and fit into unobtrusive light fittings but they can be expensive. If you buy a light that requires an unusual size or style of bulb, buy a few spares at the same time to save hassle later.

ABOVE If you need soft, warm lighting for a bedroom or living room, opaque glass globes like these are simple and elegant, and stylish enough not to need a shade.

RIGHT This inflatable plastic cone light makes use of coloured light bulbs, which you can change to alter the mood in a room.

Get the Right Light

Pendant lights

Back in the 80s the pendant light was seen as the poor relation to more sophisticated sources, such as recessed ceiling lights, but now that designers have realized that not everyone wants to take on the financial responsibility of a whole new system, they have returned to this old trouper introducing a wealth of interesting new designs to make these lights popular once again. Many rooms have just one central ceiling light which can become a focal point, so choose a lampshade that's funky as well as functional. Models that direct light upwards give a much softer light than those where the bulb is exposed from below.

RIGHT Unconventional materials and shapes characterize funky lighting.

LEFT Coloured dots are never far away in the funky home. Introduce them into your design scheme on translucent plastic.

Table lamps

No room should be without its full quota of table lamps, the most flexible kind of lighting. Ideally you should buy a size that fits the proportions of your room, and remember that the taller the lamp base, the wider the pool of light it casts. Dark shades tend to absorb light, while pale shades reflect it. Shades made from opaque materials such as plastic or card tend to give a directional light, casting shadows up or down (good for task lighting), while translucent shades made from paper or glass for example give a softer glow (better for ambient or accent lighting).

Standard (floor) lamps

Freestanding floor-level standard lamps are indispensable sources of ambient, task or accent light, while their height can add welcome variation to low furniture. Translucent shades are best for ambient lighting, and opaque for accent or task lighting. Choose lightweight, easily portable lamps for extra flexibility. A rigid standard lamp is good for up lighting walls, while flexible designs are better for reading or other close-up work

Uplighters/down lighters

These are simply terms for lights which direct light either up or down, and can be wall-mounted, freestanding on the floor or fixed onto track systems. Up- and downlighters are good for highlighting special objects or just to create a good atmosphere.

OPPOSITE Disguise ambient lights as pictures. In this apartment, exuberant flower designs are lit up from behind as the light is projected through the coloured panels.

RIGHT The artichoke lamp is made from translucent white plastic, and its severely offbeat design guarantees its standing as a focal point.

Have you got enough?

The worst thing you can do is under light a room. It may cost a bit more at the outset, but invest in good lighting – and plenty of it – and you'll have the means to change the atmosphere from warm and relaxing to bright and energizing at the flick of a switch. Unless your living space is very small, try using some of these lighting recipes as your lighting ideal:

LIVING AREA

One pendant light
Two to four uplighters
Three or four table lamps
One or two decorative lamps
Two picture lights

OFFICE/WORKROOM

One pendant light
One standard lamp
Two table lamps
One or two task lights

BEDROOM

One pendant light
Two bedside lights
Two wall lights
One or two table lamps

LEFT Funky lighting can be discrete. This dining room gets plenty of natural light during the day, and a couple of simple wall lights are all that is needed to set the tone at night.

RIGHT A slim, pretty string of tiny paper boxes is an attractive alternative to the standard reading lamp, and gives a lovely diffused light. Their versatility of form allows you to drape them, hang them, hide them, or coil them to suit yourself.

STYLE POINTERS

Small rooms can look larger and more spacious with a couple of uplighters to bathe the walls with light.

Install dimmer switchers, especially in bedrooms and living rooms.

Don't ignore natural sources of light – candles and firelight add drama and warmth to your lighting scheme.

If you work with a PC at home, make sure light shines on the keyboard rather than at the screen. Position the PC with its back to the window (and use adjustable blinds) to reduce glare.

If you use a dressing table to make up, install table or wall lights on both sides to give an even glow to your face.

Read with the pendant light dimmed down low and a lamp shining at book height.

Just a couple of sparkling white halogen lights will inject any room with a touch of glamour.

Use small light bulbs for atmospheric, strong shadows, and pearlized bulbs for a soft, more diffused light.

If you like the idea of flickering light but don't want the conventional style of candle, try this cute red candle man instead.

polypropylene lampshade

1. Cut out a rectangle of polypropylene to the length and width required to suit your lamp base.
2. Bend the polypropylene around the spider to test the extent of the overlap and ensure the shade sits firmly on the feet.
3. Holding the overlap firmly, remove the shade and rivet it at the top and bottom to secure.
4. Place it back on top of the spider, tucking one of the feet inside the overlap.

Materials

Sheets of polypropylene
Standard rivets
Rivet tools
Lamp spider
Lamp base
Scissors

TIPS If you're not confident about cutting the polypropylene immediately, or wish to try some unusual curvy shapes, experiment first with a paper template. I used a simple spider device, but you could also use a standard lampshade frame. With polypropylene, the more intense the colour, the less translucent it is when lit. Make sure you always use a low wattage bulb, as higher wattage will melt the polypropylene and ruin all your good work.

pattern
& texture

Pattern and texture are two key ways of harnessing creativity and bringing excitement into your home. This is the stage at which you can add shape and dimension to your living space, creating points of interest and defining your personal funky style. On the walls, sofa covers, curtains, throws, blinds, chairs, floors and of course accessories, you can introduce as much or as little as you like. The aim is towards extravagance – animal prints and strong geometric patterns are all dominant features. Indulge yourself with luxurious fabrics such as velvets, mohair, chenille, feathers, brocade and embroidery, and experiment with the new breed of synthetic textiles.

Using Pattern & Texture

The repetition of pattern and touch of texture bring depth and movement to a room. Ideally these elements should come after you've chosen the main colour scheme, unless you already have something you can't bear to part with, in which case you could use it as a building block of the room's design scheme. Soft furnishings are an obvious place to introduce patterns. There's no need to coordinate everything in sight, but it's a good idea to have some kind of a game plan, choosing small areas of detail that are similar in colour or tone.

Patterns

Start off by keeping things fairly simple, with perhaps just one or two patterns. You can always add to them later. If there's nothing you like more than a riot of crazy patterns and rainbow colours then go for it – as long as you don't mind the risk of over stimulation.

If you already have a highly patterned carpet or sofa for example it might need to be calmed down by a plain wall colour. If on the other hand you have indulged in paint effects on the walls you may choose to have plain soft furnishings and create interest through texture instead.

Get your use of pattern in proportion. Large scale prints can dominate a room and make it look small, while a large number of small patterns can look lost and insubstantial in a large room.

If you are not too confident about using patterns, restrict their use to small-scale items such as cushions, stools and throws that can be moved around till they find their right place.

Make use of an obvious colour scheme to link different patterns, or make use of one pattern in two or three different colours to bring a unifying element to quite a bold pattern scheme. The aim is not to overwhelm but to add interest and vitality.

Above all, get those swatches in. Beg, borrow or buy the largest possible samples and try them out alongside existing features and paint colours.

ABOVE Boldly patterned rugs create a splash of drama and these black and white numbers from Ikea interconnect, too.

RIGHT A modern version of the *Butterfly* chair which contrasts a tactile, fleecy covering against the pattern of its angular metal legs.

Funky patterns

If you'd like something completely original, rummage through lengths of retro fabrics at markets, and car boot sales. The abstract geometric shapes of the 50s and early 60s in muted shades work surprisingly well with contemporary colour palettes. If you want something more offbeat and colourful, try late 60s and early 70s psychedelia to set your pulse racing. If you don't want to use these fabrics for large-scale curtains or sofa coverings, cut and sew them into generously sized cushions covers, stool tops and table runners.

If you're unlucky in your quest for originals, make your own – Pop Art-style designs work especially well. Much of Pop Art centres around strong, bright patterns such as cartoons or recoloured photographs, so you can design your own piece of plain fabric with repeated images of your choice. Some large print shops can transfer these images onto the material (look in Yellow Pages). The images may not be completely washable, so restrict their use to decorative blinds (laminate them so they can be wiped clean), wall hangings and throws.

If you like the idea of a genuine 60s look, you could get in some fabric dyes and wax and try you hand at batik, or simply get knotting and experiment with tie-dye, both of which work well on curtains and cushion covers.

LEFT A colourful paper wall hanging can cover blemishes on the wall, adding a uniform pattern in a gradation of colour.

ABOVE RIGHT Repetitive patterns of a single image, or circles and other geometrics are very funky.

RIGHT Florals are acceptable in funky style as long as they are not too pretty.

Fabric

Natural fibres such as cotton and wool are wonderful and versatile textures to have in your home, but now that we are embracing all things synthetic – and retro – man-made fibres such as nylon and acrylic are making a big comeback, alongside innovations such as suede effect microfibres. And let's face it, they do have some solid benefits such as being colourfast and washable. That's not to say that silk, cotton, wool and linen should be forgotten – they still form the backbone of most people's soft furnishings, but these can now be supplemented with rubber, astrakhan and plastic. Opposite are just a few examples of the best of funky fabric.

Wallpaper

Funky walls are looking sophisticated and tactile, and wearing shiny, glittery and pearlized surfaces, fake wood and bamboo panels, hessian, weaves, leather and suede effect, offbeat stripes and checks. It's hard to forget the shiny sponge-clean vinyl, strangely surreal florals and ugly woodchip that gave wallpaper a bad name in the past, but the new designs and textures present a very different story. There's plenty of retro wood-effect and textured wallpaper around to please 70s revivalists, but alongside them come more modern interpretations featuring hand-painted designs, magnificent prints and futuristic photographic images. The bad news is that the best of modern wallpaper is fairly labour intensive to produce and so can be expensive, and there's still the battle of the trestle table to contend with. Still, for a touch of character and individuality in part of a room, perhaps on just one wall or an alcove, it could be a worthwhile investment.

HI-ENERGY
1. Tangerine chenille.
2. Lime chenille.
3. Fuchsia corduroy.
4. Pea green Chinese silk.

METALLIC
5. Glittery plastic.
6. Disco synthetic.
7. Bronze metallic.
8. Shiny tortoiseshell plastic.

TACTILE
9. Red matt rubber.
10. Brown textured cotton.
11. Pink astrakhan.
12. Fake snakeskin.

KITSCH
13. Shiny nylon.
14. Organza covered feathers.
15. Pink floral plastic.
16. Overblown Chinese motif on silk.

RETRO
17. Circles and roses.
18. 70s squares.
19. Homely cotton.
20. Organic patterned cotton.

ABOVE Go on, be a hedonist. Soft fleecy and knitted cushions in a harmonious blend of colours look great and are lovely to touch.

TOP RIGHT There's no reason for stools to be neglected. Have them re-covered in imitation fur just like these.

ABOVE Stepping out of a sci-fi movie, the *Bubble* chair looks wacky and can give you a massage too! Add a softer element with a quilted throw in cotton, satin or silk.

Texture

Anything tactile is a good alternative to pattern, and if you can mix different textures together for a layered luxurious look, so much the better. Cross the fluffiness of sheepskin with the warmth of knits, and the soft sheen of velvet and suede in blended colours. Keep your eyes open as well for furnishings in mohair, leather, chenille, corduroy and nubbed woollens and silks. A fur throw is a must. (See pages 80-81 for details on making one yourself.) If you don't want to go for real fur, then there is a huge range of fake varieties available that creates a similarly glamorous look.

Funky is about mixing and blending different textures to really tantalize the senses – so get carried away by contrasting plastic bubble placemats against the surface of a polished wooden table, and smooth stainless steel units against the raised relief of a metal floor. Place the luxury of natural fibres of cottons and satin alongside mass-produced furniture from man-made materials.

Colours are important too, when you consider that there are wonderful energizing dyes for fur fabrics, so that you can avoid their natural look altogether and pick something totally synthetic. Feathery throws in acid pinks can conceal an old sofa under their softness and help bring an otherwise aberrant piece of furniture into your room scheme.

RIGHT A medley of different textures – and colours – makes for a fun yet sensual feel in a room, through the contrast between the thick pile of the fake fur rug, the downy feathered appearance of the pink throw and the smoothness of the plastic table. Satin textiles add extra titillation.

Mixing pattern & texture

Create startling opposites and contrasts through your use of patterns and textures in furniture and soft furnishings, and maximize the potential of both in everything you have. Consider the inherent pattern in objects and furniture and juxtaposition of accessories. The raised texture in a rubber floor for instance creates a rhythmic pattern, and soft patterns appear in fur as they catch the light and are moved by your hand.

For a really chic look go for combinations of texture, such as smooth and rippled, fluffy and metal sleek, to add a sensual quality to your home. Alternatively be inventive with one type of pattern and incorporate texture. The circles in a blind can be mirrored in the texture of the Bubble Chair, or a bobbly rug or mat. Similarly colour can create differentiation on a theme, so that while the pattern you have chosen may be wild and funky, the effect is satisfying and calming.

The picture on the left shows sumptuous use of these two elements of home style. Pattern emerges through the contrast of the strong circular outline of the table set against the more delicate swirls of the accompanying chairs. A curved edge is also echoed in the shape of the sofa. Rich Eastern colours help to lift the overall scheme and the black and white prints of the cushions covers add a visual punch.

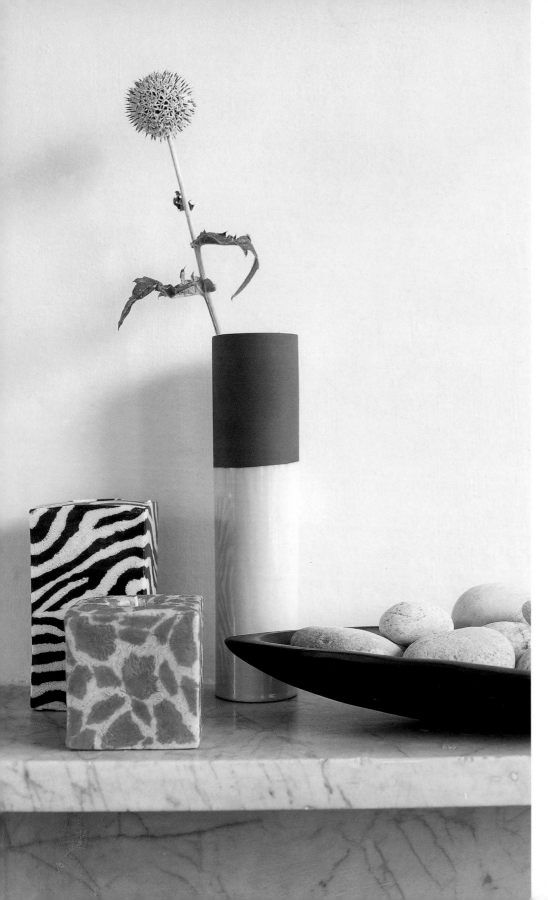

Don't use paint effects such as sponging or dragging to introduce texture to your room – they are definitely out.

Try a limited amount of the new-look wallpapers in metallic, glittery, pearlized, textured and geometric finishes.

Experiment with swatches before using more than a couple of different patterns in any one room.

Indulge yourself with as many different textures as you like – go for velvets, fake fur, feathers, fleece, knits, weaves and chenilles.

Scour second-hand shops and markets for good retro-patterned fabric that could be made into a blind, wall hanging or even laminated place mats.

ABOVE A taste of the Orient is mixed with exotic colours for these funky cushions.

LEFT Elements from the natural world are brought together in an attractive way. The animal print candles sit comfortably beside the handcrafted vase and bowl of pebbles.

fake fur throw

1 With the velvet right side up, fold the fabric at one of the corners to bring the edges of two sides together. Working back from the corner, place pins at the point where the fabric is 3.5cm/1¹/₂in across.

2 Fold the velvet along this line and pin where it touches the fabric. Machine or hand sew along this line and trim off the excess material. This will give a velvet trim of 2.5cm/1in, plus a seam allowance of 1cm/¹/₂in. Repeat steps 1 and 2 with the remaining corners.

3 Line up the straight edges of the fur and velvet exactly along one side. Machine stitch along this edge. Repeat for the three remaining sides, catching in the edge of the corners and leaving a small opening along the fourth side.

4 Turn the throw the right way out through the opening and smooth out each corner. Close up the opening with neat overhand stitching in a similar colour thread to the fabric.

Materials
1.4m/56in square of fake fur
1.5m/60in square of velvet
Sewing machine
Sewing kit

TIPS I used a thick pile fake fur, but short pile such as fake astrakhan, pony print or zebra would all look good. For the trim, felted wool, textured cotton or suede-effect microfibre are all good alternatives. The size of the corners dictates the width of the velvet trim, in this case 2.5cm/1in. It's important to get this right – the rest will follow naturally. When sewing a seam across the corners, make sure the fabric is neatly tucked down flat to avoid ruching.

windows

True funksters turn their backs on the pleated and frilly to embrace the clean, the smooth and the streamlined. Today's pared-down styling allows windows to do what they should be doing – letting in light, air and sunshine. Funky window dressing can still be colourful and even dramatic, and there is always room for gorgeous curtains, but avoid tie-backs and ruching. Sheer fabrics either in white or jewel colours, full-length curtains in stunningly patterned or textured fabrics, café-style half blinds, severe metal blinds and shutters, glass bricks and decorative finials in materials such as glass, copper, resin, leather or steel can breathe life into the most ordinary window.

Window Styling

Windows are important to funky styling both in the architectural framework that they bring to a room and also in the way that they allow natural light to filter into that room, uplifting the spirits of all who sit inside. In an ideal world, where privacy is guaranteed for all, and cold winter nights don't make us want to draw inside and shut the world out, we would leave our windows unadorned to accentuate their shape, possibly painting them in a shade of the wall colour. But the treatment of your windows through structure, pattern or one of the other methods mentioned in this chapter can all allow you to be as creative at the window as you are in the other decorating elements of you home style. If you don't know where to start, make sure your blinds and curtains fit in with the rest of the room's theme. Coordinating them with the colour of your paintwork or the upholstery is a reliable starting point.

Ready-made curtains

Ready-made curtains are affordable and easy to source and fit, especially the kind with tab tops that you simply slip over a curtain pole. Don't skimp if you go for this option – buy curtains that are at least one and a half times the width of your window. Equally, buy long rather than short, as any excess can always be draped artistically over the floor or even chopped off to make cushions. If you do have to give your curtains a short back and sides, leave a good deep hem that will add a little weight to the bottom of the fabric, allowing it to hang smoothly.

LEFT A blind echoes the design of the louvred cupboard door for a cool modern bathroom.

Where there's room, fit a curtain pole that extends a reasonable length at the sides to accommodate each curtain when it is pulled back. This will reduce the amount of light being blocked by the curtains during the daytime. If you like to add you own imaginative touches to plain ready-mades, you could sew points of interest such as eyelets, buttons, beads, raffia, tiny bells, shells or anything else that catches your eye. If you like quite a dramatic look for your windows, use two layered curtains for extra versatility, one fine and one thick. The thicker one can be drawn back in the summer. Add subtle character to full-length curtains by putting in two or three horizontal pleats near the bottom.

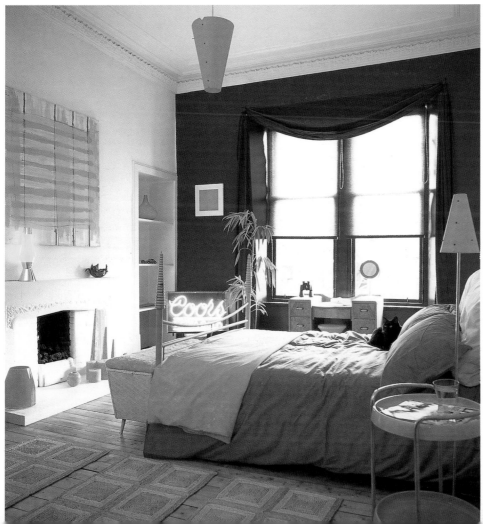

ABOVE These full-length Ikea curtains boast a wild pattern which is picked up in the circular pattern of the rug, while the floor cushions bring a whole new meaning to the word co-ordinated. Not for the fainthearted, but it makes a tremendous impact.

LEFT A draped dark blue curtain frames the window and merges with the blue of the walls and window recess for a contemporary look. Blinds can be pulled down for privacy.

Make your own

If standard fabric curtains aren't what you want, try some of the following simple and cheap alternatives.

Make your own blind from any kind of funky fabric, including rubber and plastic (see pages 74–75), perhaps in an interesting shape, then have it laminated so it stays that way.

Use fine muslin or other sheer fabric to keep out prying eyes but let in the light.

If the idea of sewing makes you feel queasy, source lengths of groovy fabric, fold over a hem and press flat, and attach to your curtain pole with curtain clips.

Try putting a tall screen in front of a window instead of curtains or blinds.

Dye good quality cotton sheets in bright, hi-energy colours and hang them up with curtain clips for an easy modern look.

Buy lengths of silk or even sari and drape them overlapping onto a pole for a luxurious and exotic look.

If you want to make your own blinds, linen, hessian and canvas don't necessarily need lining.

If roller blinds are your choice, add detail with a pelmet made from the same fabric or in a contrasting colour, and trim the edges with a narrow border in a different shade.

Use steel mesh (the kind for screen doors) as a shiny metal blind. Tuck in any sharp edges and simply pin it neatly to the window frame using steel or aluminium pins.

If it's flat, you can make a blind from it. Sheets of wood veneer, millinery straw, handmade decorative paper, sheets of MDF, strips of bamboo, sheets of Perspex or even giant leaves can all be strung up from a piece of dowelling or pinned to a pole with bulldog clips. Encase them in an opaque fabric such as organza if you like, or get them laminated.

Make your own simple curtains from lengths of muslin or organza and add pockets of Perspex to colour the light coming in. Hem the sides and the top, and sew a channel at the top to thread through curtain wire or dowelling, or use curtain clips. (See pages 90–91 for details.)

If you are making curtains for the first time remember to make sure the pattern and warp and weft run in the same direction.

CURTAIN POLES
Curtain poles don't have to be wood – wrought iron, glass and bronze are all effective, and can be topped off with decorative finials.

For a cheap and cheerful curtain pole, spray a broom handle with metallic brass or copper paint or use a length of piping.

As an industrial style alternative, replace conventional poles with high-tension steel wires. You can then clip on your blinds with crocodile clips or even safety pins.

LEFT Sheer sari fabric looks beautiful, lets in light and can be easily draped over a simple curtain pole.

RIGHT Hang your hand-made curtain with peg rings over a Perspex rod.

Alternatives

CUSTOMIZED GLASS

The easiest way to customize plain windows is by turning them opaque with a special etching spray, available from hardware stores. Make your own stencil (letters, patterns, etc.), stick them lightly to the window with spray mount, then spray over the top with several coats of glass etch spray. When completely dry, carefully remove the stencils to reveal the clear glass motifs on a stylish frosted glass background.

FROSTED GLASS

Get a sophisticated sandblasted effect by sticking self adhesive frosted film, available from stationers and print suppliers, over your windows. You can cut out your own pattern using a scalpel.

Stick tracing or tissue paper over the glass for a colourful and opaque effect. Use strips of different colours for added interest, or paint on a pattern with metallic paint.

STAINED GLASS

Make your own stained glass. Draw on a simple pattern with indelible marker pen and go over it with ready-to-stick window lead, which comes in an easily dispensable roll. Paint each section with coloured glass paint.

Alternatively you can cheat and simply draw your pattern onto a sheet of acetate the same size as your window, paint with black outliner that comes directly from a fine-nozzled tube, and fill in the pattern with glass paint. Attach the sheet to the window with spray mount adhesive.

Another way of creating a colourful stained-glass effect is to use long-lasting self-adhesive sheets of vinyl (available from specialist suppliers), either translucent or opaque. Clean the window thoroughly with methylated spirits and allow to dry before peeling off the backing paper from the vinyl and sticking onto your window.

GLASS BRICKS

Glass bricks, once jealously guarded by builders and architects, have now become freely available to the creative public. They provide a wonderful alternative to ordinary glass windows, lending a functional modernity that is also immensely practical as they are tough, durable and easy to work with. Because they really are bricks (typically around 8cm/2in thick) and hollow in the middle, they offer great insulation from cold, heat and noise. Standard glass bricks are square, transparent and very affordable; hand over a few more readies and you can get your hands on dazzling colours such as turquoise, pink, red, cobalt blue, pale green and yellow in different sizes. A few enterprising bathroom

LEFT Hang a glass-beaded curtain at the window to keep out prying eyes, yet let light shine in.

and kitchen suppliers sell glass bricks with interesting textures such as ripples, bubbles and waves, and patterned or opaque finishes. If you're good at DIY – or know someone who is – you could have a go at replacing a conventional window with a solid panel of glass bricks, although this does require a certain amount of know-how about things such as load-bearing and waterproofing. If you're not exactly handy with a tool kit, then cheat – simply pile up an assortment of glass bricks on the windowsill so that they fit across the width of the window. You don't necessarily need to place them the full height of the window, half way up is plenty. Choose different colours and sizes for an abstract effect, and place a couple of coloured glass vases on top. Then sit back and admire as the light shines through the different colours and pools on the floor or ceiling.

THIS PAGE Window treatments include self-adhesive vinyl, glass bricks and metal shutters.

SHUTTERS

Shutters are a great alternative to blinds or curtains. Apart from being immensely stylish, they let the light in when folded back, help keep out the cold or heat and and offer good security when bolted. You can have them made to order by a carpenter, or large DIY stores sell the components ready to paint and hang yourself. Alternatively, try salvage yards and second-hand shops for period shutters – look out especially for the louvred kind with slats that open and close to keep out the cold and nosy neighbours. Half height shutters have the advantage of letting in the light during the day but maintain your privacy. If you fancy making your own, wood or MDF are good materials, or you could try Perspex, which is easy to work with and comes in lots of different colours.

stained-glass blind

1 Cut the muslin so that when folded in half with the selvedges running down one side, it fits the width and drop of the window with a 1cm/^{1}/$_2$in seam allowance.

2 Working on the reverse of the fabric, pin the cut edges of one side of the muslin together starting about an inch down from the fold. Machine sew a neat straight seam along this edge and along the bottom of the blind. Turn the fabric the right way out and press with a warm iron.

3 Cut rectangles of coloured polypropylene to the size of your choice and experiment with their positioning on the surface of the blind. Then mark the pockets with tacking thread. Sew three-sided pockets through both sides of the fabric with invisible thread. Remove the tacking.

4 Tuck the polypropylene rectangles into the pockets, entering the blind through the selvedge. Insert hooks in the window frame and hang the blind by pushing the dowel through the fold in the fabric.

Materials

Muslin to fit window
Sheets of coloured
  polypropylene
Scissors or stanley knife
Sewing machine
  or sewing kit
Invisible thread
Dressmaker's chalk or pencil
Ruler
Iron
Small decorative hooks
Piece of dowel for hanging

TIPS Use postcards, dried flowers and leaves, sheets of fluorescent or hologram card, and festive decorations or small flickering lights at Christmas as alternatives to the polypropylene. Use pure cotton muslin (rather than a polycotton mix) for a crisp, clean look. Use a stiffening spray for a more rigid effect. The muslin needs to be sheer enough to be translucent, but strong enough to bear the weight of the sheets of polypropylene.

furniture

Furniture may give you somewhere to sit and lounge on, but just as important is the style statement it makes, and every piece you own ought to say something loud and clear. It is worth remembering that the desirables of today are the collectibles of tomorrow, so the design ethos of funky furniture is key, whether you buy new or second hand. Shop for reinvented or original twentieth-century classics – designs that were considered progressive in their day. Hunt out items with shiny steel and aluminium frames, chrome trims, moulded plastic, seasoned leather or plywood seats, or select modern bulky shapes in hi-energy colours to create a powerful focal point in your lounge, dining room or bedroom.

Funky Classics

Funky furniture takes inspiration from the fun and the functional, and embraces both updated classics in modern materials and innovative new styles that break all design barriers. The quality (and therefore the longevity) of design is the linchpin, and it is very telling just how much of furniture around today first made its way into our living rooms way back in the 50s and 60s. The funky look is more connected to the Modernist movement of the 20s, post-War utility styling and the experimental designs of the 60s than, say, Victoriana. The elaborately carved wood, cheap pine, stuffed upholstery that were popular until recently have given way to more understated, streamlined designs that have their origins in the machine age revolution.

Look out particularly for cultural icons – furniture designs that broke new ground in materials, principles and techniques – from the big names of the twentieth century such as Alvar Aalto, Ludwig Mies van der Rohe and Le Corbusier of the 1920s, Arne Jacobsen, Charles and Ray Eames, Eero Saarinen and Robin and Lucienne Day from the 1950s and Gaetano Pesce and Verner Panton of the 1960s. If you can source (and afford) an original item, so much the better, but as mass production has given everyone access to quality design at affordable prices in a way that would have gladdened the hearts of Charles Eames *et al*, there's no excuse not to be funky. Stick to the following classics, and you can't go wrong.

RIGHT This stacking chair of 1960 was the first ever one-piece, cantilevered, moulded plastic chair. It was designed by Verner Panton, a Danish architect and designer, famous for his space-age, futuristic, curved chairs, sofas and lights.

This modern sofa harks back to the 50s, when the first mass-produced furniture was simple and organic in design and economical to produce – a departure from the cumbersome look of the pre-War years.

Asymmetric, streamlined designs in shocking colours, such as this elegant sofa, characterize the funky look.

LEFT One of Ludwig Mies van der Rohe's most celebrated furniture designs, the *Barcelona* chair (on the left) was first made in 1929 for an eponymous exhibition and is still made today by Knoll Associates in the USA.

The design of the *Ant* chair, first produced *c.*1950 by Arne Jacobsen, has encouraged many imitations, including this modern interpretation. Danish architect and designer Jacobsen is best known for his designs using the new and exciting materials of the 50s such as moulded plywood, aluminum and fibreglass. The *Egg* (see page 92) is another best-seller still in production.

The *Grand Confort* armchair is a Le Corbusier design. This radical Swiss-born architect was arguably the most influential and revolutionary designer of the twentieth century. Working in Paris during the 20s with his wife Charlotte Perriand, he produced many furniture designs that have become icons. Look out also for the B301 with bent tubular steel frame, calfskin seat and back and slung leather arms and the ergonomically designed B306 chaise-longue, both of 1928.

One of the first designers to produce organic designs, Finnish-born Eero Saarinen is famous for the Tulip table (c.1955). Originals were made in moulded fibreglass, but modern updates are often made from metal or wood. The table is accompanied by chairs with the same characteristic single pedestal foot: Saarinen's objective of the design was to clean up the 'slum of legs' in domestic interiors. Both this design and his Womb chair stand as landmarks in furniture design.

It may not look comfortable, but this Mexican chair certainly looks great, and its form evokes the welded steel rod construction chairs of Charles and Ray Eames, and Harry Bertoia.

Inflatable chairs first came into fashion in the 60s, and are a good solution to providing extra seating in a hurry. This black version is stylish too.

The Balzac armchair and ottoman (1991) is indicative of the work of British designer Matthew Hilton, which marries modernist principles with traditional furniture-making techniques. This piece is named after the French author Honoré de Balzac whose work explores the relationship between society and the human condition.

Moulded plywood became a popular material for furniture after aeronautical industry experiments during the Second World War. It was pioneered by Charles Eames, among others, in an attempt to produce organic, sculptural shapes inexpensively. This birch plywood stool by Corin Mellor is a modern take on a classic idea.

A perfect design to fall back on. The ubiquitous brown leather armchair can adorn any setting, whether modern or period, and exudes connotations of comfiness, reliability and style.

Pouffes are in, and no funky home should be without them. This one in brown suede is ideal for anyone wishing to create their childhood of the 70s.

A contemporary design that hints back to the organic shapes of the 60s, this coffee table has plenty of practical storage space as well as looking fabulous.

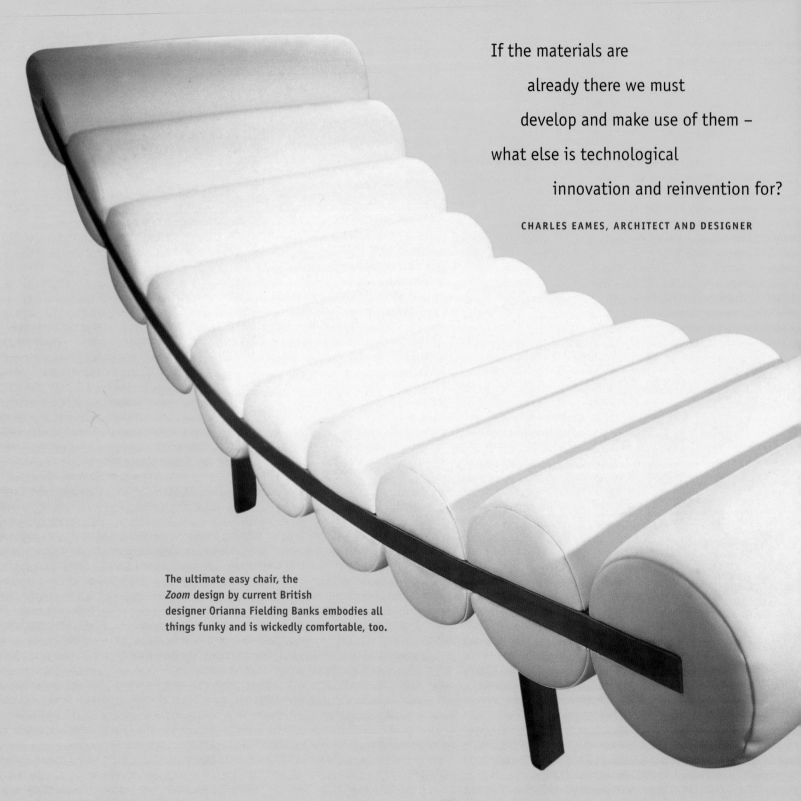

If the materials are
already there we must
develop and make use of them –
what else is technological
innovation and reinvention for?

CHARLES EAMES, ARCHITECT AND DESIGNER

The ultimate easy chair, the
Zoom design by current British
designer Orianna Fielding Banks embodies all
things funky and is wickedly comfortable, too.

A modern version of the *Butterfly* chair, originally created in 1938 by the Argentinian design group Bonnet, Kurchan, and Ferrari-Hardoy. It was distributed globally by Knoll – a US company devoted exclusively to modern designs – in the 50s and became a much-copied best-seller.

Collecting funky classics

If you want to collect in earnest, buy or borrow a history or directory of twentieth-century furniture design and read it from cover to cover. Scour junk shops and auctions for old leather armchairs, swivel chairs, stacking stools and chairs, smoked glass coffee tables, old medicine cabinets, office and school furniture. Hang around houses that are being refurbished and salvage old fixtures and fittings, or better still, consult builders working on warehouse conversions or apartment developments from former schools, hospitals, or municipal buildings. They may well be throwing out industrial fittings including lights, radiators, trolleys, blinds and sanitaryware. Commerical refurbishments can also yield covetable 60s and 70s office furniture in

unusual shades of orange, green and beige. And remember, Eames chairs have graced many a school and public hall, so you never know what you might find.

It can sometimes be hard to tell whether an item you like is an 'original' or not, as so many modern classics have been in continuous (though slightly modified) production since they were first designed, and most don't carry special insignia. But if your heart is set on an early model, your best route is to do what museum curators try to do, and buy it directly from the person who bought it first time round, and has guarded it ever since. Ask around, read the small advertisements in newspapers and magazines, or if you're desperate, advertise yourself. It is always worth browsing around specialist shops

selling twentieth-century classics as a starting point, although they can carry higher price tags. Once you have an idea of the going rate of items by your favourite designer you could try your luck at an auction, but be prepared to bid against keen collectors and traders.

If your decision is to buy new, go for streamlined, curvilinear items in subtle colours that will still look good and stylish in years to come. Visit reputable chain stores whose furniture may be mass-produced but is still based on solid design values and aesthetic appeal. If you can afford it, buy your furniture from shops and galleries that play host to innovative designers. You may end up paying a little more today, but in turn you could pick an antique of tomorrow.

Sculptor Isamu Noguchi pursued a biomorphic look with his furniture designs. His free-form glass-top coffee table (c.1944) is a much-copied classic design.

ABOVE An ordinary table can be transformed with a new top made from zinc sheeting.

BELOW Industrial chic comes into the bedroom with a bed head made from scaffolding pieces.

Customizing furniture

You could also get experimental and customize furniture yourself. Old-fashioned haberdashers, hardware stores, stationers, Oriental stores and artists' suppliers can be rich sources of unusual paint, finishes, trimmings and paper.

Spray or paint tables and chairs with silver or bronze for a sleek contemporary metallic look, or if you're handy with tools, use soft, flexible zinc sheeting (from large metal merchants) as splashbacks and covers for tables or chair seats.

Arm yourself with a staple gun and cover chairs, and stools with patterned and textured fabrics .

If you have an odd piece of wood or metal furniture that doesn't fit in with the rest of your room, paint it in a colour a couple of shades deeper than your walls.

Vamp up old stools or chairs with a new seat made from the fluffiest, deepest fake fur or shagpile. (See following pages for details.)

Update old chairs or circular tables by removing the seat or centre and replacing it with frosted, textured or coloured glass (toughened of course), cut to size by a glazier.

Go for a fake 70s look with a coat of wood-effect paint on smaller pieces of furniture such as cabinets, stools or boxes.

Add your own handles in stainless steel, chrome, brass or brightly-coloured plastic.

RIGHT Office filing cabinets make smart storage units. Clean them up, give them a coat of paint if necessary and add some typed labels.

A few practicalities

If you buy 50s or 60s fibreglass chairs, handle them carefully, as they are very brittle.

Be environmentally aware – some modern furniture is made from tropical hardwoods sourced from endangered forests. Before you buy, even if the store claims the wood comes from managed forests, check that the supplier has a seal of approval from a reputable environmental organization.

If you are buying kitchen or dining chairs second hand, measure the height of the seat from the floor and make sure it is compatible with your table, if you want to avoid knees on chins or worse still, chins on tables!

Leather and plastic furniture is brilliantly stylish, and a practical choice if you have young children, as it is durable and easy to clean, although spillages should be wiped off immediately as they can sometimes stain.

Take a tape measure with you when you're shopping for furniture, and make sure you know the dimensions for your rooms, doors and hallways to avoid expensive mistakes.

fluffy stool

1   Make a template by placing some plain paper on top of the seat and drawing around the edge. Cut around the pencil outline. (The template does not have to be exact.)

2   Pin the template to the reverse side of the sheepskin and cut around it including a generous allowance for the thickness of the stool and the seam.

3   Hem stitch a firm seam all the way around the seat cover leaving enough space for the elastic to run and a gap through which to thread it.

4   Cut a length of elastic that will fit snugly around the underside of the stool seat and attach the safety pin to one end. Thread it through the seam allowance via the gap (make sure you don't lose the other end). Pull the two ends tight, evenly distributing the gather of the skeepskin. Test the seat cover over the stool, and when satisfied that it sits tight enough, tie the two ends in a secure knot and cut off any excess elastic.

Materials

Sugar pink Mongolian sheepskin

Thin elastic

Sewing thread and needle

Scissors

Plain paper

Pencil

Safety pin

TIPS I used a loose, long-piled sheepskin, but you could use any kind of fleece, although the fluffiest varieties give the softest, most bouffant seat. If you plan to use the stool frequently, make sure you choose something hardwearing such as sheepskin. Watch out too, that the fleece you choose isn't prone to losing lots of fibres. If your stool seat doesn't already have padding, insert a thick layer of kapok under the fleece to give added height and bounce.

flexible living

Being funky means being mobile and flexible, ready to change and adapt your actions, mood, home and style instantly in response to practical demands from your environment. So make the most of your living space, and look out for streamlined modular storage units and furniture, anything on wheels, and storage cubes, as well as freestanding vertical shelving. It is great to have an eclectic and vibrant home, and mixing the kitsch, the classic, and the old is positively de rigueur, but it doesn't mean displaying everything you've ever owned. As ever, it is a case of less is more, so unless you naturally incline towards the minimalist or live in a palace, selectivity and smart storage are paramount.

Maximize Your Living Space

Ever since Alvar Aalto pioneered his famous stacking stool back in the 20s we've been looking for design solutions to maximize our living space. Some eighty years on, more of us live in single-occupancy households than ever before, and city dwellers have pretty much got used to the limited environment of modern-day apartments. Our lifestyle has become all the more hectic, too: we get up, perhaps do a speedy exercise routine, hurry off to work, dash home to quickly prepare some tasty food, have a few friends to dinner, then off to bed – all in the space of a few hours. More and more people are working from home, and even for those who do travel to an office to work, there is often a need for a small office area at home. For many people it is compact living – eating, sleeping, entertaining, working and watching TV in just a few rooms. Life is busy, life is pressured and life is full, and we need our homes to be arranged as efficiently as possible to make it run smoothly and painlessly, whilst at the same time keeping our sense of aesthetics razor sharp. So lose the surplus clutter, store (or better still give away) what you don't need and introduce some furniture that is slim, pared-down and above all flexible.

LEFT We all need some version of a home office. By using strong, clean designs for your office furniture, you can set it up discreetly in the corner of the room, and the furniture pieces can be borrowed for other needs when required.

One handy flexible basic is a good quality sofa bed. It doesn't have to be huge, but it does need to be as good for sleeping on as for sitting, so look for a sturdy steel frame and a proper sprung mattress, plus a folding mechanism that is smooth and easy to operate. A foam-filled sofa bed will suffice, but bear in mind the filling may become compacted and less comfortable after a year or two, and it will start to lose its shape.

A good alternative is a futon – but try and lie before you buy as the firm surface is not to everyone's taste. If space is really tight, you can buy a futon as a 'bed in a bag', which is simply a thin rolled-up mattress that stores in its own neat kit bag. And for extra sitting and sleeping arrangements that can be completely stored away out of sight when not needed, buy an inflatable bed, armchair or sofa – along with a sturdy pump.

Other living and storage necessities are catered for by a wide range of innovative furniture that combines great design with strong storage potential. Roughly they fall into four main categories – multi-function, metamorphic, mobility and utility.

ABOVE For an instant bed invest in the inflatable mattress, which deflates to almost nothing and can be stored on a shelf. Some, like this model, come with their own rechargeable electric pump for blowing it up.

BELOW If your place is the size of a shoe box and friends still insist on sleeping over, this bed in a bag futon must be the most compact way of accommodating them. It may not guarantee a perfect night's sleep, but it's affordable.

Multi-function

There is a huge range of dual-purpose furniture produced today that is well designed and stylish, and can allow you to keep down the amount of furniture items in your home to give you a greater sense of space. Look out for sofas and armchairs with book sleeves incorporated into the arms, low-slung tables with an internal shelf or mini drawer, and blanket boxes and ottomans that double up as seats, all of which will enable you to store small items out of sight.

BELOW A chic white leather couch can assume the appearance of a single bed, by removing the cushions for the back and arms.

RIGHT A shelf unit can be used to display objects or to hide them away in sturdy utilitarian boxes.

LEFT Storage cubes can be used individually as small tables for drinks and snacks, or they can be stacked and used as a bookshelf.

RIGHT A superb multifunctional unit is the trustworthy chest. You can use it as a table, a seat, and to store away the spare bedding and blankets for the sofa bed.

Metamorphic

The fun and the functional finds its best expression in the furniture that can be taken apart and re-formed to make something else. Tables that can become seats, chaise longues that can be transformed into beds, and other clever items can completely alter the look and role of a room, which is so helpful in our times when rooms often have dual roles. The unusual forms and arresting colours that characterize the new designs can add dramatic flair to your living area, while keeping the overall look clean and clutter-free.

RIGHT It looks like a pouffe, can be used as a table and can be taken apart to make some wildly interesting floor seating.

ABOVE According to your needs, this piece of furniture can be either a table or a bench. Use the cushions for lounging on the floor.

RIGHT With a hinged back, this chair can be converted into a stool or small coffee table. With their simple design the stools can also be stacked in the corner, out of the way.

ABOVE An ingenious take on the idea of nesting tables. The units can be stacked as one table, separated into three, placed upside down on top of each other to make an unusual bookcase, or on their side as an interesting sculpture.

BELOW It's made from suede, it's the colour of decadent dark chocolate, and it's totally gorgeous. The *Cicero* day bed can be lounged upon by day, but it can also be transformed into a bed at night to impress your sleep-over guests.

ABOVE This cabinet on wheels brings a modern look to freestanding furniture.

Mobility

Wheeled items in lightweight materials give you flexibility with style. Storage units can be wheeled against walls, or moved into place as a temporary screens to divide two separate areas. Trolleys can be moved around the house, or taken outside for serving drinks or food. Stacking stools and folding chairs can be stored in cupboards or against a wall and brought out for extra guests, as can beanbags and floor cushions, perfect for low-level chilling out.

ABOVE This versatile trolley table adds a little industrial chic

BELOW A tall shelf unit on castors can be used to display accessories, and can be moved into place as a room divider.

RIGHT A low coffee table can be moved around to suit your needs. If you own a bed on legs, you could also wheel this unit underneath.

BELOW Bring out cool white floor cushions, which match any colour scheme, when you need some extra seating.

BELOW Get a couple of inflatable armchairs that can be moved from room to room.

Utility

Form follows function in the funky home. If something has been bought to serve a purpose, there is no reason why its utilitarian nature shouldn't be reflected in the design. Storage items can still look pleasing if they have simple lines and use quality materials with little unnecessary surface decoration.

ABOVE Moulded plastic stacking chairs are versatile informal seating.

LEFT Tall slender shelving is perfect for slotting into recesses or tight spaces.

BELOW LEFT This coffee table can be extended and moved around depending on the shape of the room.

BELOW Translucent plastic drawers are undeniably stylish, and allow you to glimpse the items you are storing.

RIGHT Tall, slim lockers make ideal storage and add a splash of colour. If you're lucky enough to pick up one second hand, sand it down and give it a coat of spray or acrylic paint to get a similar effect.

Hide it

It is one of those strange laws of physics that the number of possessions (read clutter) you own always expands to fit the amount of space you live in. Under the bed, under the stairs, in the cellar, loft, garage, shed, on shelves, in cupboards or simply in piles in a corner of the room, we all have 'stuff' that we don't necessarily use on a daily basis but refuse to throw out on the grounds that 'it may be useful one day'.

Not everyone subscribes to a feng shui or minimalist lifestyle, but we can all afford to do a little sorting and pruning. After all, a heavy dose of clutter is horrible to look at and unsettling when it surrounds you. So discard as much of the surplus as you can bear to, and stack the remainder as neatly as you can in some attractive and imaginative storage facility from the range of ideas in this chapter. (See pages 116–117 for a simple storage box.) This will leave you more space to display your finest funky furniture and accessories, and for the important things in life, such as having friends round, doing yoga or simply stretching your legs out a bit more.

If you can't zap it, then hide it behind a screen. You can buy wooden ones made out of MDF that come ready to paint, or you could make one up with four lengths of timber (roughly 50 × 50mm/2 × 2in width) screwed together with small L-shaped brackets to form a rectangular frame. Cover with fabric tacked lightly to the back or staplegunned in place. Make two, three or four panels (use different coloured fabric if you like – using some ideas from pages 74–75) and hinge them together. Mount them on castors for portability.

ABOVE One minute it's a chair, the next it's a single bed. The leather *Convenio* sofa has considerably more style than an ordinary futon, and is easy to convert.

Create the illusion

When the room is small, a pair of compact two-seater sofas (one could be a sofa bed) is more balanced than a bulky three-seater option.

A plain day bed (narrow, no arms, no folding mechanism) covered with scatter cushions looks good enough to be a couch during the day, but converts without hassle into a bed at night. Store bedding underneath in a shallow box or wheeled drawer.

For clean, modern lines that help maximize all available space, go for reflective and clear materials such as steel, chrome, glass and Perspex.

Choose streamlined furniture with slender legs that leave plenty of floor showing rather than squat, bulky items.

Make use of large mirrors to create the illusion of space, but don't go over the top or your house could end up looking like a fun fair.

Add castors to freestanding furniture so that it can be hidden under worktops if things get crowded.

When floorspace is tight, think vertical. Inexpensive plywood boxes lined up in a vertical row look good. Leave them bare, or paint them the same colour as the wall.

Make use of 'dead' areas under the stairs, above a doorway, on the landing, or at the top of the hallway. Use them for storage, for a desk or to fit a cupboard. Invest in an extra large cupboard with a swivel-out shelf that can double as a work station for your computer.

customized boxes

Materials

Shoe box

Scissors

Fablon or sticky-backed paper

Pencil

Ruler

Decorative feathers, stickers, photos or even plastic fish!

TIPS I used fake wood effect for this storage box for a groovy 70s effect, but any strong decorative paper will do. Make sure your shoe boxes are in good condition, as any defects will cause the paper to crease.

1 Using the grid on the reverse of the Fablon as a guide, place the box on its side and mark a piece to fit with a 2cm/³/₄in overlap at each of the four sides.

2 Cut out the paper around the pencilled markings.

3 Carefully peel away the back of the paper and stick down firmly on one side of the box, smoothing out air bubbles with your fingertips and pressing down the overlaps. Repeat for the other side of the box.

4 Mark out and cut a piece of Fablon that exactly fits the width of one end, with overlaps at the top and bottom. Peel away the back of the paper and stick down securely over one end, smoothing out air bubbles and pressing down the overlap onto the bottom of the box and over the lip. Repeat for the other end of the box. For the lid: mark and cut two pieces of Fablon for the two ends of the lid, with overlaps at all four sides. Peel away the back of the paper and stick down as before. Mark and cut a piece to cover right across the width of the box with an overlap at the two sides and stick down as before. For a decorative touch, add plastic fish, stickers or photos.

accessories

You've painted your walls, chosen your furniture and laid down your funky flooring, so now comes the fun part – the accessories that help a room leap into life and give it that stamp of individuality. Whatever you're into, this eclectic look can be home to almost any kind of decorative detail from the downright outrageous to the ultra classic. So anything goes, but look out especially for ephemera from the 50s, 60s and 70s. Even the 80s can be cool. Slender wavy vases, abstract art, Pop Art (the real thing or contemporary imitation), big architectural plants and unusual flowers, bright plastic containers of all kinds, colourful glassware, hi-energy gadgets and appliances, anything kitsch and homemade or customized pictures all have a place.

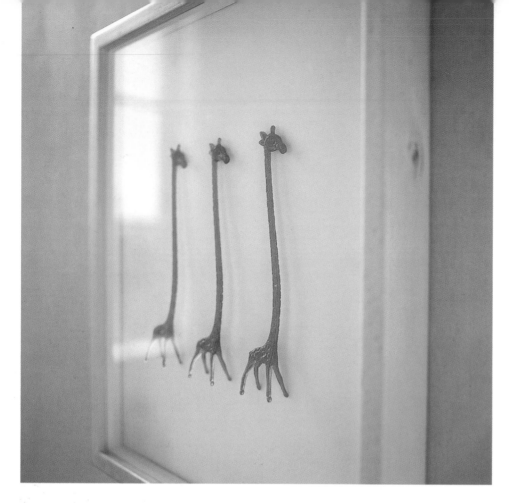

Displaying Accessories

Once you've put the basics into action, and your place is looking more like a cool pad, it's time to think about the finer details. Your much-loved accumulation of pictures, rugs, kitchen appliances, throws, office gadgets, cushions and ephemera are things that you have collected during the course of your life and make your home something you've created personally. But don't just collect for the sake of it – you only need around half the accessories you think you do. It's far more effective to display fewer but better quality items. For the funky home, it is worth seeking items that are less mainstream.

When you're happy with your choice of accessories, it's nice to display them in a place that's reasonably accessible and at a level where they can be seen easily. Don't get too obsessed about lining things up in rows or making everything the same height – funky is not about being finicky. On the other hand, a minimum amount of organization can help.

Spend some time considering which items work well together in terms of colour and shape. If you have a particular collection that takes pride of place in your heart, think about the best way to show it to best advantage. For instance, football or baseball cards can be pegged onto thin wire with small clips and hung across a wall, or pinned together to make a lampshade. Large pictures can hang on their own to form a focal point, but small and medium pictures have more

ABOVE & LEFT Make your own pictures with a plain inexpensive frame and a little imagination. One shows a row of plastic giraffe cocktail stirrers; the other a child's hand print.

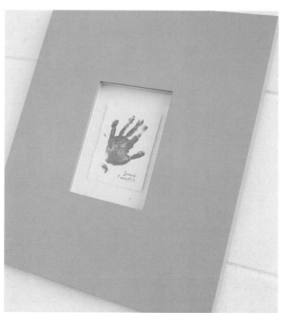

impact grouped together, especially if all their frames are different. If the frames are identical you could hang them together in a line or square. Hang the largest picture first and arrange the others around it (experiment by arranging them on the floor first if you like) and keep the look fairly random – don't worry about getting the distance between each one exactly equal. If your walls aren't as straight as they could be, hanging them over a swathe of sheer fabric that hangs down to the floor helps hide faults. If your rooms are small, put larger pictures or groups in a hallway or landing so they don't dominate.

Large, wide picture frames with a tiny centre or chunky box frames are both stylish ways to display oddments. Try an interesting leaf, a colourful, kitsch glass ornament, a fiery-red chilli, a square of textured or handmade paper, one or two feathers on a background of tissue paper or perhaps a row of three shapely shells. A vertical or horizontal row of wall-mounted wooden cubes is a good way to display larger nick-nacks.

You don't have to invest in real art, bought from galleries with huge sums of money. Try car boot sales or garage sales, auctions, charity shops and markets for affordable collectibles like 70s coloured glassware, old posters, 50s lamps, slim-line 60s pottery or other unusual oddments. Or try and discover the next funky icon by haunting student graduation shows and local art exhibitions where you can often buy paintings, sculpture, ceramics, collages and metalwork at competitive rates.

LEFT Storage cubes stacked off-centre can be decorated with all kinds of bits and pieces, from coloured glassware to a collection of dolls.

BELOW An old metal cabinet stripped of paint and polished is a great way to display a prized collection of CDs or clocks – especially when it sits alongside Arne Jacobsen's classic *Ant* dining chair.

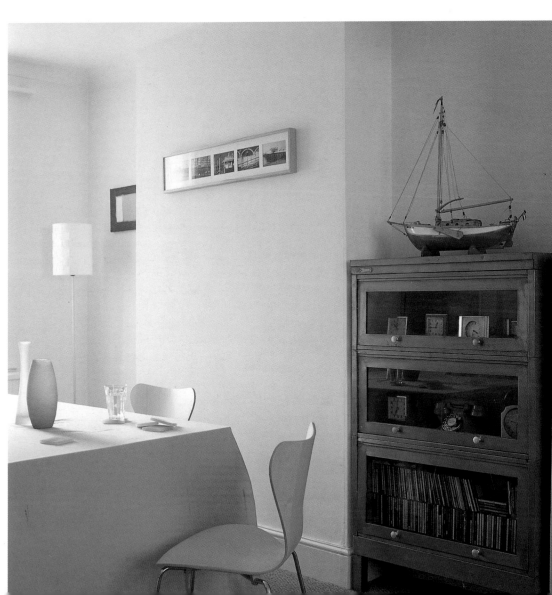

Accessorizing when cash is tight

You don't have to spend a fortune for an instant update. Try some of these ideas:

Revamp your crockery. Go for plain white in a classic style. Alternatively, source 70s-style geometric patterns or get something square in a subtle colour from bric-a-brac market stalls, car boot or garage sales.

Change your light switches to coloured shiny or pearlized metal.

Change handles on doors, drawers, light pulls and cistern flushers.

Take a long hard look at your lighting, and invest in a few sleek new table lamps for an instant improvement.

Hide ugly bits and pieces in inexpensive funky storage boxes or jars.

A small pile of interesting or pure white pebbles makes the ultimate in cheap accessories, and sprayed in silver they are really hip. Heap them on a windowsill, a mantelpiece, in a clean fireplace or a clear glass vase.

Assortments of ill-matched accessories, such as picture frames, small vases or candle holders that otherwise look odd or out of synch can be painted or sprayed all the same colour. Pearlized or metallic paints, especially bronze and chrome effect, work well for this.

Customize plain glass shelves. Use a gift wrap motif as a template and place it underneath the glass shelf on a table. Copy over the design using a small paintbrush dipped in water-based varnish. Spray glass etch spray over the shelf and it will become opaque, except for the varnished patterned areas.

Turn up the heat with red-hot chilli peppers and fake tomato plants (*solanum*) in old tins for a gutsy South American look.

If you don't like table cloths, make runners instead that go from one side of the table to the other from deckchair decking or brilliantly coloured paper.

Install a Perspex shelf above a radiator to protect walls from discoloration and paint radiators the same colour as your walls.

Customize plain lampshades or picture frames by sticking old sheets of music, maps, ordinary brown paper or unusual gift wrap over the surface so they overlap, wait until the whole thing is dry, then give them a coat of clear water-based varnish. Or create an abstract pattern by splattering them randomly with emulsion paint, stick embroidered motifs over the surface with strong glue or a length of gold bead fringing around the base (this works best on cylindrical-shaped lampshades).

Flower-arrange the modern way. Paint a piece of board in different colours and stick on glass test tubes with strong adhesive. Half fill these with water and add a thin-stemmed bloom.

Make good use of old sweaters and turn them into one-off touchy-feely cushion covers. Simply put a cushion pad inside a roomy pullover, trim away the excess and sew a firm seam all the way round.

If you haven't the time or the money for fresh blooms, fake it with silk: big bunches of overblown silk roses, artfully arranged Japanese cherry blossom or just two sprays of white orchids.

Immerse bright green marsh grass in a galvanized bucket.

Place half a dozen thin, tapering candles at random in a boxy container filled with fine sand for soft, diffused light.

TRY A CHIC INDUSTRIAL LOOK: measure the centre panel of your kitchen cabinet doors and get a metal merchant to cut a piece of stainless steel to the same size. Use a super strength adhesive to glue each one in place. Alternatively, you could use sheets of tough acrylic or Perspex in bright colours from a specialist supplier. Drill holes in each corner and simply screw them in.

Stick a rectangle of funky giftwrap exactly over the centre panel of each kitchen cupboard door, and seal it with two coats of clear, quick drying varnish.

Replace kitchen cupboards with safety glass.

Install some stainless steel shelving in your kitchen to complement shiny appliances.

Make splashbacks and table tops for the kitchen and bathroom from toughened safety glass, stainless steel or zinc.

Make transfers of your favourite images and stick them onto your cupboards. Seal with a coat of clear quick drying varnish. Take a photo of your favourite family member or pet, or just a still life to a print or photographic services store that offers a copying service.

Brightly coloured or frosted glass wall tiles make funky place settings or coasters for drinks.

Place mats can be funky – make your own from colourful or kitsch giftwrap overlaid with different images and then laminated, or pick a couple of your top photos and take them to a photographic or printing shop and make them into place mats. (You can do this for mouse mats, too.)

DINNER PARTIES: Make your own place settings out of offcuts of wood and coloured paper. (See pages 126–127 for details.)

Buy paper labels, write the name of each guest and attach them to wine glasses with clothes pegs.

Use luggage labels as place cards, tie decorative tape through the holes and write guests' names in gold or silver ink.

Place just the head of a gerbera or other wide-bloomed flower across each plate for a splash of colour, or stand a single Michaelmas daisy in a plain glass by each person's place.

Wind colourful raffia around the stem of each wine glass and tie the ends in a bow.

Tie cutlery placings for table settings together with beads or sweets on elastic.

Make simple table runners with white tissue paper, and stamp a design onto the surface with a rubber stamp dipped in metallic paint.

GO GREEN: There's nothing like a bold plant to add a touch of bio-drama to your living space – think big, bad and spiky.

If you have limited space, go for a quirky row of cacti lined up on a long, low table.

Go retro with a few Swiss cheese plants or self-cloning spider plants that are a throwback to the 70s. For something a little more restrained, small mounded or trailing plants closely planted in galvanized metal buckets are low maintenance and stylish.

Hide cheap terracotta pots inside interestingly textured raffia baskets or bright plastic laundry bins, or paint them indigo or silver.

Put sunflowers in a decorative tin, Chinese lanterns (*physalis*) in a hollowed-out butternut squash, ornamental cabbage leaves in a hessian-wrapped pot or artichoke flowers in a clear long-stemmed vase. Try *ranunculus* in an opaque glass vase, pompom-shaped *alliums* in a silver container, or a couple of canna for an exotic touch of the jungle.

Knot together half a dozen vermilion *amaryllis* stalks with raffia and set in a chunky red glass vase.

LEFT It's tall, eye-catching and funky, and it ought to be right there in your living room. With plants like this one, you won't need much else as accessories.

RIGHT It may look like a UFO, but this is actually an inflatable fruit bowl. The ideal overseas funky Christmas present.

place settings

1 Mark the centre of the wood with a small cross made by placing the ruler across the diagonals from corner to corner.

2 Drill a hole around $^1/_2$-1cm/$^1/_4$in deep.

3 Make a fine slit at the top of the dowel long enough to accommodate the label with the stanley knife.

4 Push the dowel firmly into the hole until it is secure. Write and cut a coloured label and tuck it in place at the top of the dowel. Use a different colour for each setting.

Materials

Square of wood, approximately 8cm/3$^1/_4$in across and 2cm/$^3/_4$in deep

Electric or hand drill with drill bit size of 6$^1/_4$

5mm/$^3/_{16}$in dowel approximately 15cm/6in long

Sandpaper

Stanley knife or scalpel

Pencil

Coloured card and pen for labels

TIPS Use different kinds of materials for the label – transparent acrylic, shiny metallic or textured paper for example. Experiment with different inks such as fluorescent and glittery. If you prefer something more decorative, paint or spray the wood in bright coloured or metallic paint.

creating the look

Perhaps you're in the lucky position of having a totally blank canvas of a room, or more likely you've got several bits and pieces and a whole load of ideas about the way you'd like to get seriously funky. Either way, now is the time to step back and think about how all the different elements could work together. A little planning goes a long way, and even if you gave up drawing way back in junior school, a few basic sketches or plans, plus paint swatches, tear sheets, photos and fabric samples can help you get going and avoid heart-breaking mistakes.

The Look For You

Given the choice, many of us would probably begin our home-making efforts with a huge, totally empty room boasting vast windows, clean white walls, a superb fireplace and gleaming beech floor, where all that's needed is a swipe of a paintbrush. Into this you could add a few choice pieces of furniture and a few treasured possessions. It's nice to fantasize about how you'd get going on achieving that ultimate funky look given the perfect empty setting, but let's face it, not many of us have such gorgeously advantageous beginnings.

If you have, then all well and good, but you're more likely to start off with an average-sized room with several items of furniture that you can't afford to change, or drab flooring that has to stay down for the foreseeable future. Yet the worst thing you can do is compromise, using existing unsatisfactory furniture and accessories as the initial building blocks. If you're a hundred per cent happy with what you've got then that's fabulous – you can build on that. But if you have a suspicion that Gran's cast-off couch in 'autumn leaves' fabric isn't quite your thing, then stop right there. There is always a quick solution to problems such as these. Old sofas can have a dramatic shape to them which may be in keeping with the funky ethos. You can easily cover faded or ugly fabrics with a throw (or sew two together if the offending item is a biggie), and piles of cushions.

LEFT Sugar pink is the perfect backdrop to a kitsch bedroom, in which a whole medley of different styles co-habit chaotically but happily. Sheepskin, raffia, feathers and zebra prints add fun, fluff and texture, while brazen floral curtains cling to the very edge of the taste scale.

RIGHT For a restrained retro look the design of this room combines family heirlooms with bold designs in black leather and chrome.

BELOW Modern meets classic in this room which combines a few large, expensive pieces with smaller trinkets to fabulous effect, such as the intriguing modern light in the fireplace with the antique French mirror. The round table is a Charles Eames design.

Place a brightly coloured rug over dingy carpets, paint over dark, unattractive wooden furniture, or rescue strangely coloured curtains by dying them in the washing machine.

If you decide that something's truly beyond redemption, take it to your local recycling centre or charity shop – it may fit someone else's funky scheme. With this in mind when you're on a tight budget, it is always worth going to have a browse through the second-hand shops yourself to see if there isn't anything there with lots of potential for you to work some magic with a staple gun, sewing machine or paintbrush.

The basics

Firstly you need to decide on the overall look you want to achieve – whether it is kitsch, retro, or classic. This will help to bring a satisfying cohesion to your style. The pictures on pages 130, 131 and 132 all show a different slant on the funky theme. See which one appeals to you most.

Once you have a clear picture of how you want the room to look you need to think about the dynamics – how people will move around it, whether you need to watch television, is it OK for social occasions; and the practicalities – where will you put the TV, VCR and CD player, items of furniture; and how these will fit in with existing features such as recesses, windows, fireplaces and doors.

Once you've got rid of anything you don't like or need, you can use whatever is left over as the basis for your room scheme, perhaps taking the colour of a piece of furniture as a starting point for your wall, ceiling and paint work colours. If your not sure about combining colours, you could try one the following examples for instant success.

WARM

Warm colours are very easy to work and live with, and centre around brown and pink-based shades such as chocolate, coffee, burnt orange, almond, amber and ochre, with sage green, soft grey and sludgy blue as less obvious alternatives. Warm colours are ideal for rooms where the light is dull, and for the current mood of 70s styling.

 aubergine & mustard

 Wedgwood blue & milk chocolate

 cranberry & ocean blue

COOL

Cool, pale colours are easy to co-ordinate and make for low-stress colour scheming. They help you relax and are perfect for people who hate clutter and mess. Look for chalky shades that are gentle on the eye such as watery blues, greys, aquas, off whites and light beiges.

 taupe & chalk white

 sage & gooseberry

 lilac & violet

REFRESHING

If it's an early morning wake-up call you're after, or a room to instill energy, go for fresh, clean colours with plenty of light in them. Be confident and combine fruity sorbet shades, raspberry, Caribbean turquoise and zesty citrus colours such as lime or orange.

 strawberry icecream & lime

 orange sorbet & honeysuckle

 turquoise & fuchsia

VIVID

If it's an impact you crave, choose deep, intense colours undiluted by much white pigment. Purple, scarlet, cornflower yellow, midnight blue, these are colours for confident decorators who reject neutrals in favour of drama and electricity.

 flame & tangerine

 sugar pink & scarlet

 mulberry & Pacific blue

Layout

A simple scale plan of the room (try 2cm for every 20cm/1in for every foot) should help you decide where to place things and if space is a problem, may throw up some space saving solutions.

Try some of the following:

SMALL NARROW ROOMS
A slim sofa against the longest wall and a couple of ottomans in front should maximize the space available, particularly if the ottomans can also be used for storage. Low, narrow shelving could sit directly opposite the sofa.

STRANGELY SHAPED ROOMS
Try placing a low table in the middle of the room with the seating grouped around informally rather than against the wall to minimize awkward dimensions.

SMALL ROOMS
Try placing the sofa far from the door to minimize its impact and give some floor space as you enter the room.

BOX-SHAPED ROOMS
Try two small sofas placed at right angles to each other with an additional armchair if there's room. If there are alcoves, use them for storage, and keep tables as low as possible.

Getting a focal point

Every room needs a focal point, but what it is should be up to you. Obviously, if there is something in the room already, such as a full-length window or amazing fireplace, then that should be enough, but otherwise you need to create it. Try an impressive floor lamp or ceiling light, or an oversize vase full of flowers, or let the furniture do the talking with a beautiful sculptured sofa or table. A stunning mirror also makes an easy focal point. If you have a plain one, you could try transforming it with glass etch spray with an original design so that it really grabs attention when people enter the room. (See pages 138–139 for details.)

Ideally you should wait for the room to evolve rather than trying to make it work immediately, and you will find that a focal point may naturally emerge. The best thing about the funky look is its versatility, so try re-arranging the furniture to create a new focal point every now and then.

Misuse, reuse, abuse.
Stash your kitchen in a tool trolley,
put industrial pallets on
floors and walls.
Be bold, be big,
use strong shape and colour.

TOM DIXON, DESIGNER

Using a storyboard

You've decided on the look you are after, you've considered and planned the layout, bearing in mind your potential focal point, and you've thought about the colour scheme. Now is the time to really narrow down your choice of paint and upholstery colours, the flooring, trimmings and details. A storyboard is a really useful tool to help you experiment with different swatches and ideas, and visualize how they will work alongside each other.

Use a large piece of white card or mounting board to display paint chips, fabrics swatches, thread, trimming, piping, flooring and worktop samples to see exactly how colours, finishes and textures look together. Annotate your storyboard with notes on where you sourced the particular swatches and what area of furnishing or decorating they relate to.

If you are having trouble choosing between more than one colour or finish, put both on the storyboard – the chances are that once you see everything together one choice will look better than another, and so you can eliminate as you go along. Use generously sized samples, roughly in proportion to their usage in the room, and keep introducing new ones until your instinct tells you it's just right.

Steal other people's ideas by collecting tear sheets from home interiors magazines that appeal to you. If you're on a budget, try to be realistic – total up roughly how much you think it's all going to cost, then add about another 20 per cent on top to cover unexpected contingencies.

The storyboard opposite outlines a modern, low-key scheme for a living room with a small kitchen area to one side, and centres around light, subtle colours, the minimum of pattern and paint with a soft sheen – all designed to maximize the light and make the space look larger. The funky element comes through in the choice of textures and materials. The colour palette is limited but warm-hued, and is therefore easy on the eye and simple to work with.

Ready for change

The great thing about funky living is that it is all about going with the flow. So when your mood changes, you can change the furniture around; when you get bored with the colours, you can re-paint the walls; a couple of unexpected guests turn up, and you can alter the layout of the room to make it more sociable. It's all about achieving a fluid yet dynamic living environment. So spend time with a few key elements before you go all out for that final funky look.

UPHOLSTERY FABRICS

CUSHIONS OR PIPED EDGES

CURTAIN/BLIND FABRICS

FORMICA SAMPLES FOR KITCHEN SURFACES

FRENDENBURG RUBBER FOR KITCHEN FLOOR

WALL 1

WALL EMULSION PAINTS

FLOOR PAINT COLOURS

WALL 2

EDGING SAMPLES

acid-etched mirror

1 Place your mirror (upside down to protect it) onto a large sheet of paper and draw around it with a pencil.

2 Remove the mirror. Keeping within this outline, draw a random shape for the design to use as a stencil. Don't worry about making it too neat, the more curly and swirly the better. Cut out this shape. Working in a well ventilated area, place the mirror right side up on sheets of newspaper. Spray mount your paper stencil, leave to dry for a few seconds and press it down firmly into position on the surface of the mirror.

3 Holding the can of glass etch about 15cm/6in away from the surface of the mirror, spray the exposed area of the mirror evenly. Give it two or three coats for a smooth finish. Leave to dry.

4 Gently peel off the paper stencil. Any small marks can be easily removed with lighter fuel and a soft cloth.

Materials

Mirror
Glass etch spray
Spray Mount or Sellotape
Large sheet of paper
Scissors
Pencil or pen
Newspaper

TIPS Glass etch spray is available from large DIY stores and artists' suppliers. Always read the instructions on the can before commencing. You can use the spray on lots of glass objects including wine glasses, windows, bowls, vases and paperweights, but note that the finish is not intended to be dishwasher proof. If you decide to have a mirror cut to order for this project, ask for its edges to be bevelled as this looks so much neater.

Picture credits

All project photography, and the photographs on pages 42-43, 48, 74-75, 95, 136-137 were taken specially for the book by Chris Tubbs.

Other photography reproduced by kind permission:
Livingetc magazine, (listed by photographer):
44 Photography pp20, 22, 24 (bottom), 66, 70, 118; Peter Aprahamian pp26, 29, 31, 33, 39, 40 (left), 49, 64 (middle), 85 (bottom), 121 (bottom), 122, 128, 131 (bottom), 132; Graham Duddridge pp65, 94; Polly Eltes p106; Craig Knowles p120; Hannah Lewis p53; Tom Leighton pp55 (right), 76 (top right), 86, 103, 108; Jonathan Pilkington p96; Nick Pope p114; Ed Reeve pp7, 134; Tom Stewart pp6, 32, 61, 76 (bottom right), 79, 130; Chris Tubbs pp24 (top), 28, 30, 40 (right), 42, 46, 48, 58, 60 (bottom), 73 (left), 74, 76 (left), 84, 95, 136; Simon Watts pp38 (left), 121 (top); Verity Welstead pp50, 77; Polly Wreford pp3, 25, 52, 55 (left), 67, 82, 87, 88, 89, 131 (top).

Cut out photography by David Barrett, Mark Grimwade, Lee Hind, Moonlight Photographic, Bill Osment, PSC, Mel Yates

Colour magazine and Dulux pp36 and 41
    (photographer James Merrell)
Earl Carter/Belle/Arcaid p18
Mathmos Ltd p63
Matthew Bailey p115
Nick Crosbie p125
Paint Library p38 (top)
Pure Contemporary Design p100
Richard Waite/Arcaid p92
room magazine p85 (top) (photographer Richard
    Powers);

The 'Nuta' stool for the fluffy stool project was supplied by Purves & Purves, 83 Tottenham Court Road, London W1.

Project index

Index

First published in 1999 by Ward Lock
Illustrated Division
The Orion Publishing Group
Wellington House
125 Strand
London WC2R 0BB

Livingetc is published eleven times per year by
IPC Magazines Limited, Kings Reach Tower,
Stamford Street, London SE1 9LS. For subscription
enquiries and orders please call 01444 445555
(fax no: 01444 445599). For credit card orders call
the subscription credit card hotline (UK orders
only) on 01622 778778.

ISBN: 0-70637-868-7

Series Editor: Ljiljana Ortolja-Baird
Editor: Alison Moss
Designers: LewisHallam
Projects Photographer: Chris Tubbs
Steps Photographer: Rodney Forte
Projects Stylist: Lucy Gibbons